JAPANESE DOLLS

JAPANESE DOLLS

THE IMAGE AND THE MOTIF
JAPANESE DOLLS

LEA BATEN

Shufunotomo Co., Ltd.

Tokyo, Japan

Acknowledgements

My first and greatest debt I owe to my photographer-son, Jackie Borromeo, who with Asian patience and cheerfulness, put up with my exacting demands on his time and talents. That this book was written is due to his encouragement and his steadfast faith in me. His photography is more than illustrative—it is a personal vision of the doll motif, expressed by a sensitive interpreter. I thank my daughter Ann for her labour of love—she typed the manuscript and gave unstintingly of her time and typewriter ribbon.

—To Raymond Bushell, collector and photographer, I am indebted for the loan of transparencies representing doll *netsuke* from his world-famous collection. He is an ever helpful and courteous gentleman, who is never appealed to in vain.
—To Miss Eiko Oyama, who with gracious Japanese hospitality and kindness, permitted photography of rare pieces from her collection.
—To Amaury Saint-Gilles for his advice—contemporary Japanese art has no more devoted promotor. I am privileged to have him as a friend.
—To Harumi Yoshizawa and Nariaki Suzuki for help with translation problems.
—To Jessie and Luc Sanders for access to their collection and documentation.
—To Kazuhiko Nagai and Michiko Kinoshita respectively manager and editor of Shufuno-tomo's International Department, who, from the start, showed understanding and sympathy for my project, and did all they could to promote my rather unorthodox view of an intriguing subject.
—To all the collectors, art gallery owners, antique dealers, artists and friends who helped and encouraged me, and made this book a truly international endeavour.

Reading over my manuscript, I realize that my book is far from perfect, far from complete. It is not a learned treatise, it is a pleasant ramble through Japanese art and history, an eclectic collection of dolls, objects, documents and stories with a common factor: the doll image seen by artists and craftsmen. Museum pieces are absent—they can be seen in their glass cases, many have been repeatedly portrayed in other books—and, above all, they are not collectible. I hope I have illustrated fully that the principal doll theme leads to many side paths that are worth exploring—motifs worth collecting. If this book has given interesting reading and tempted anyone to look beneath the surface of simple things, I will feel amply rewarded for my work.

Pupil: Latin pupilla—diminutive of pupa—doll—the tiny image of oneself seen reflected in another's eye.
(Webster's Seventh New Collegiate Dictionary)

For any deformation of the image during reflection I am strictly responsable.
For the realization of my wish I am indebted to Daruma and have presented him with a second eye.

Contents

Part II: THE MOTIF

Part III: MISCELLANEA

Introduction

That weighty mountain of wisdom and knowledge, the revered Encyclopaedia Britannica, says, with due caution: "Perhaps" the oldest plaything of mankind. We are informed that dolls dating from 3000–2000 B.C. carved of flat pieces of wood, geometrically painted, with hair made of strings of clay or of wooden beads, have been found in Egyptian graves and that a fragment of an alabaster doll from Babylon, with movable arms has been recovered. The Bible tells us that God made man from clay "to His own image and likeness"—and so, from the beginning of time, man has felt the need to create images, to be a creator also. Reflected in the image does he not recognize his own ability to conceive and give form to a thing of beauty and power? What is art, but the magic of creators?

How many of us when asked—what is a doll?—will not immediately reply—a child's plaything, usually in the form of a baby or a small human figure. In Japan one must definitely contradict the first part of this definition. It is certainly everything except a child's toy. It is a god, a hero, an emperor, an empress, an amulet. It can be a religious sculpture, a decorative statuette, a treasured family heirloom, a souvenir, an art object. If children enjoy dolls, it is only visually. An analogy exists between the setting out of the European Christmas stable complete with all its accessories and the Girls' Day display of the Imperial Court with all its trappings.

The Japanese doll has many functions: it is a healer of illnesses, a giver of health and fertility, a granter of wishes; helped by the doctor it gives an easy childbirth, aided by the bank and hard work it will make you rich—it will even help your sons and daughters through their difficult examination period! It has the elevated status of a work of art when made by a "Living National Treasure", it is a humble folkcraft artifact when made by the anonymous artisan. No country in the world is as rich in the most varied types of dolls as Japan, they are a unique expression of Japanese culture. The natural materials are as different and abundant as the dolls: clay, wood, paper, textiles, and lacquer.

Here it must be mentally underlined that the Japanese word *ningyō* which today has the general meaning of doll, and by extension, different kinds of playthings, derives from the Chinese characters 人-*nin*: human, person, 形-*gyō*: form, image. The same characters in their earliest interpretation read *hitogata* or divine shape…And there is yet another definition: *nin*=man, *gyo*=fish—merman or mermaid—mythological beings—reality, religion, magic, and myth. Of these themes is given an interpretation in its broadest sense; mostly dolls and the doll motif, but also some religious images; fact, fiction, and a few fantasies.

I would like to put up a warning board "For eclectic collectors only". Admittedly I am an eclectic collector, I have no pretensions to great expertise (my experience lies in the domain of exhibitions). My saving grace is love of beauty and "things Japanese". For me collecting only dolls would be like planting flowers of the same shape and colour in my garden. Like Sei Shōnagon I collected (doll) motifs for my personal "musée d'images". I collected what I liked and what interested me; and because any art object stays somehow incomplete unless its history is known, I also collected stories. I was well rewarded, for the doll led me along unknown paths and to unexplored perspectives. It was not so much the idea of the doll as a decorative object or plaything, but the symbolism of the human figure and the magic of the fetish that intrigued me. An artist lives on in his creations, and his art, by some subtle magic, becomes an intermediary, a bridge spanning the centuries. It is wonderful that if we are receptive enough, we can still receive messages sent out many years ago. The spark is always there, Ariadne's thread leading us through the labyrinth, to true beauty and spiritual gain.

When I visited Japan for the first time I was given a contemporary, unclothed young lady, who is not yet dressed, because she is so beautiful in her structural simplicity. The two large old Kokeshi dolls I took home with me were under suspicion at every customs counter. From there I was caught in the *ningyō* "image" and the deep meaning it holds in Japan. I was always happy to find an interesting and unknown aspect of a subject, which I had taken for granted, while ignoring its true essence and thankful to the artists who gave me a renewed vision. A porcelain bowl told me about Imari and Tachibina, a metal clasp about pouches, pipes and puppets, an actor print about Kabuki and wood-block pictures. Murasaki Shikibu who wrote *"The Tale of Genji"*, Japan's greatest classical novel, between 1008 and 1020 A.D. did not forget to mention innocent dolls and a dolls' house, used as instruments of seduction; that famous lady of crime and mystery, Agatha Christie, wrote a little known short story entitled *"The Dressmaker's Doll"* in which a malefic doll becomes harmless when it is picked up and cherished by a slum child—because all it had ever wanted was to be loved. These are two roles I hope my dolls will fill—to seduce and to be loved...but my motives are pure...

Through the whole cultural history of Japan the doll motif lies entwined like a pale silk thread. The doll seems too humble an object to have any importance on an entire socio-cultural background and is generally not mentioned in the history of a country—and yet the imprint is there—the representation of the history and religious beliefs, superstitions and folk customs, amusements and even fashions of a nation. The pictorial and written image is important because it reflects the entire aesthetic and spiritual development of peoples. We enrich our environment with the concrete images of artists, we enrich our spirits with the philosophies of the greatest minds. Yet when we leave the museum, we may also visit the fair, and after reading G.B. Shaw, we can enjoy our children's comics. While aspiring to higher things, our childhood still lives and echoes, as the marvels of the great unknown world of adults beckoned when we were young and we became aware of the realities of life, both beautiful and cruel. The precious gift of childhood which the lover of beauty conserves is the gift of wonder, of admiration, the sudden realization that a line has a certain rhythm, that proportions are harmonious, that a bird's feather is a masterpiece of complexity, that perfection lies in the grey and white surfaces of a winter horizon or the curve of a voluptuously rounded tea-bowl. And so the motifs are forever interwoven, the human figure, man-made artifacts and the beauty of nature. The totem pole rises above a village, the scarecrow stretches protecting arms above the fragile seedlings and the ripening crop. Jizō guards travellers, roads and children. Children build snowmen. Adults make images. The image is the symbol of a reality and its role is to remind us what it stands for: religious, concrete or spiritual, it permits a passage, a communication between this world, the human, and a higher dimension, the divine. Human, it is a link between the world of the past and the present moment. It is a condensed memory of all that has existed during the ascent of man. Remembrance is the only immortality we know and can pass on to others.

Many things in Japan are made only to be looked at, not to be touched or caressed as one is naturally inclined to do with beautiful things. The false rusticity of the tea ceremony, where the old Chinese tea-bowl and the signed bamboo tea-scoop can be worth a small fortune, where a few simple flowers are arranged with the taste and refinement inherent to centuries of culture—creates an atmosphere that can only be sensed with the antennae of the spirit, but not held fast. Thus the butterfly—see how exquisite, how fragile, how perfect in its living beauty—but do not try to capture, to keep it. The result is pitiful. So the beautiful garden is made to be looked at, to become THE garden—absorbed by the eye and stored in the mind. This reflection is immutable and one can always reach into its peace and its serenity—it has become an image. Enter the image-garden of Japanese art, a strange landscape made of ivory and lacquer, porcelain and silk, paper and iron, heroes and dolls—look carefully at all these things, then turn them over in your mind, gently, like fragile, precious things—and in your mind's mirror you will SEE ripples on a pond in an endless transparency, you will HEAR the rustle of silk behind a paper screen, you will SMELL the perfume of gardenias at twilight, you will FEEL the dripping bamboo in the rain, you will TASTE warm saké in tiny ceramic cups in winter. Your garden does not exist tangibly and yet you possess it for ever.

A Short and General Survey

The paleolithic Age ca 30,000 to 10,000 years ago, also named The Pre-Ceramic Age.

The people were hunters and gatherers, used fire, and lived in pit-type dwellings or caves. They had no knowledge of pottery and used chipped stone tools. They wore animal skins.

Dogu

Two Neolithic Cultures: Jōmon and Yayoi
Jōmon: 10,000 years ago until 250 B.C.

Jōmon 'coiled rope' or 'cord marks' took its name from the particular pottery found at excavation sites throughout Japan. It was made with coils of clay and said to be inspired by basketwork. It was hand-formed and of powerful and elaborate execution.

Dwellings were grouped, clothing consisted of animal skin and vegetable fibre. There was jewelry made of seashells, bone and horn. A large number of clay figurines, 'dogū', magical objects associated with fertility cults, have been excavated.

Yayoi: 250 B.C. to A.D. 250

Yayoi pottery was wheel turned, fired at higher temperatures for practical use. Metal was known. In agriculture the wet cultivation of rice was practised. At this time there was an influx of Korean immigrants, bringing Chinese methods from the four Chinese colonies in Korea, such as primitive loom weaving. The dead were buried in clay urns and stone coffins.

# of Japanese History

Proto-historic or Kofun Period: AD 250–552

Kofun or Tumulus is named for the tumuli or man-made mounds over the stone coffins of important people. Haniwa 'clay circle' figures were placed in and around the tombs. These models of human beings and animals were made until Buddhism came to Japan in the 6th century. Horse sacrifice was banned. States governed by powerful clans came into being. Yamato (Japan) possessed tributary states in Korea.

Haniwa

Asuka or Suiko: 552–646

Buddhism was introduced through Korea (Paekche) around 552. With Buddhism came Korean scholars and artisans. The Chinese calendar and ideographic script were adopted. The Prince Regent Shōtoku Taishi wrote a basic law, *"The Seventeen Article Convention"* in 604, stipulating the rights and duties of Ruler, Ministers and People. The Hōryū-ji, the oldest existing wooden building was erected in 607.

Nara: 646–794

The establishment of the capital at Nara in 710, built on the Chinese model of Ch'ang-an, went together with a great propagation of Buddhist religious art, visibly influenced by Confucianism and T'ang styles. The late Nara period became known as the Golden Age of Japanese sculpture. The Emperor Shōmu and his consort Kōmyō were fervent Buddhists and promoted the construction of many temples, the Great Buddha in the Tōdai-ji, and the Shōsō-in, the oldest treasure repository of Chinese objects and of the art works of the late Nara period. Emperor Shōmu also invited the Chinese prelate Ganjin to come to Japan. He succeeded after six attempts, but became blind. The *'Kojiki'* (Records of Ancient Matters) 712, and *'Nihongi'* (Chronicles of Japan) 720, were compiled.

Buddha

Jizo

Heian or Fujiwara: 794–1185

The Emperor Kammu moved the capital to Heiankyō or Kyoto, to cut the ties between government and Buddhism, which had become too influential. The capital was again laid out on the plan of Ch'ang-an. In the 10th century developed a truly Japanese culture. An indigenous script, the *kana* syllabary, appeared, and with it two world-famous literary achievements, *"The Tale of Genji"* by Murasaki Shikibu and Sei Shōnagon's *"Pillow Book"*. New Buddhist sects were introduced: Tendai Buddhism by Saichō and Shingon Buddhism by Kūkai. The Fujiwara ministers dominated in the 10th and 11th centuries and the Emperor became a symbol without effective power. All art forms flourished and there was great technical mastery in the execution of ceramics, metalwork, lacquer, and textiles. There was a clash for power between two powerful clans, the Taira and the Minamoto (Heiji war, 1159), in which the latter were defeated. The Buddhist monks abandoned pacifism and took to arms. The Taira clan was crushed in 1185 and Minamoto-no-Yoritomo became Shōgun or military ruler. Kyoto stayed the imperial capital from 794 until 1868, the time of the Meiji restoration.

Kamakura: 1185–1338

Kamakura became the military capital. The accent was on sobriety and simplicity. Zen art, known in Japan since the Nara period, therefore became much appreciated. It was the age of worship of the sword. The great Buddha of Kamakura was completed in 1255. After Yoritomo's death, his wife's family—the Hōjō—took power as regents for the Shōgun. Mongol invaders were twice repulsed: in 1274 and in 1281, their fleet destroyed by typhoons or 'divine winds'. These attacks resulted in isolation from China until the 14th century. From 1336 to 1392, there were two imperial courts; a northern (Kyoto) and a southern (Yoshino) court—both pretenders to an empty throne without power.

Ashikaga or Muromachi: 1338–1568

The Ashikaga Shōguns returned to Kyoto and succeeded in reuniting the two dissident courts. They were men of taste, patrons of the arts and they inaugurated a new cultural era. This period is named after the Muromachi district of Kyoto where the third Shōgun, Yoshimitsu built his palace. He also built the Kinkaku-ji or Golden Pavilion, to retire and live the life of a priest, while still exercising great influence. The eighth Ashikaga successor, Yoshimasa built the Ginkaku-ji or Silver Pavilion, and neglected all affairs of state for aesthetic pursuits— he was a great amateur of the arts of the tea ceremony. Zen art in all its forms was much appreciated—landscape gardens, paintings, flower arrangement, ceramic, lacquer and metalwork all carry the mark of this extremely refined and rich period. The so-called Higashi-yama culture (country estate of Yoshimasa) has been called the forerunner of the brilliant Azuchi-Momoyama and Edo cultures. From the agricultural festival dances, Noh developed. The father and son Kan'ami and Zeami emerged from the guilds attached to the Kasuga Shrine and the Kōfuku-ji, and laid the foundations for the classical Noh drama. The last century of this period is one of civil war.

Tachibina

Momoyama: 1568–1615

Three men stood out against the troubled background of civil strife, serving as stepping stones for the next phase of Japanese history—unification and peace. Begin, continuation and achievement. Oda Nobunaga, the initiator was assassinated in 1582. His general, Toyotomi Hideyoshi, in power from 1582 to 1598, continued the process and invaded Korea twice (unsuccessfully—1592 and 1597), built Momoyama Castle at Fushimi in 1594 and brought Korean potters to Japan. Tokugawa Ieyasu (1542–1616), spent seventeen years in the struggle for supreme power over Japan...and succeeded.

Artistically the short Momoyama period was fertile in innovations.

Gosho

The newly built castles and strongholds called for brilliant and impressive interior decoration. Quiet refinement and Zen were forgotten in the baroque splendour of gold and silver screens, colourful and asymmetrical paintings and many kinds of radiant lacquer objects.

Tokugawa or Edo: 1615–1868

The famous and decisive battle of Sekigahara in 1600, established Ieyasu's supremacy over Japan, and his descendants maintained power for nearly 300 years, isolated from the rest of the world. Ieyasu again separated the military capital from Kyoto and moved to Edo, a small village which has grown into the modern Tokyo. Christianity was introduced in the 16th century by Spanish and Portuguese missionaries. The Shōguns feared their militaristic intent and saw the significance of firearms. Forbidden since 1612, Christianity was banned entirely after the peasant uprising at Shimabara in 1637. Foreign trade was prohibited and foreigners were expulsed, except for a few Dutch and Chinese merchants on the closely guarded island of Deshima, off Nagasaki. Japanese could not travel abroad. Edo became a growing capital and, as such, attracted all kinds of merchants and artisans, willing to work and make their fortunes: in a few decades all economic power was in their hands. In the late 18th century, Edo with its more than one million inhabitants was the largest and most densely populated city in the world. As always in Japan, the peasants and farmers were the exploited and they remained poor. In the cities sumptuary laws aimed at restriction of wealth, but many ways were invented to circumvent them. The rich wanted to live, live well, and enjoy the good things of life. They wanted to be entertained, to possess fine clothes and objects. They became literate and read books and wrote poetry. They could now afford to patronize celebrated artists. Names, famous in Japanese arts, emerge: Kōrin, Kenzan, Buson...the great master of *haiku* verse, Bashō. All the facets of a bustling, busy city show in the wood-block prints of Moronobu, Harunobu, Sharaku, Utamaro, Hokusai, Hiroshige; the Kabuki actors, the puppet theatre, the women of the Yoshiwara, the

Nara

Uji

Kamo

Saga

sumō wrestlers, the landscapes inviting travel...the first popular art...

Tengudani, possibly the first kiln to produce porcelain in Japan, was established in Arita by Koreans (1616). Kakiemon, Imari or Arita ware, Nabeshima, Hirado, Kutani and Satsuma, range from masterpieces to mass products. Metalwork, from simple and elegant to rich and flamboyant; especially evident in *tsuba* and sword furnishings, in pouch and purse clasps, is the unique, Japanese manner of using the tones of metals to their best advantage. The richness and variety of textiles and techniques are admirable—silk, brocade, cotton, weaving, embroidery, tie-and-stencil-dyeing, painting. Wood-block prints testify that a woman's kimono, obi, and hair ornaments were her most beautiful and costly possessions. For men, wearing a sobre, if costly kimono, the claim to fashion lay in the miniature masterpieces called *netsuke* and *inrō*, both of which can be pretenders to the greatest choice of subject matter, material, treatment, and pure, inventive genius.

Ichimatsu

Kokeshi

Meiji: 1868–1912

Then came Admiral Perry in 1854, and opened Japan to the West and Western influence...the last Tokugawa Shōgun relinquished his office in 1868, and the 'Enlightened Rule' of Emperor Mutsuhito began... The ban on Christianism was lifted in 1873 and 'hidden Christians' were found in Western Kyushu and some small islands. It was a period of adaptation and imitation, artistically not often to the advantage of Japan, economically a game quickly learned and won. Thousands of *netsuke, okimono* and wood-block prints found their way to foreign countries, as the first examples of the strange and fascinating art of the Land of the Rising Sun. The Past is always Prologue...

Kobe

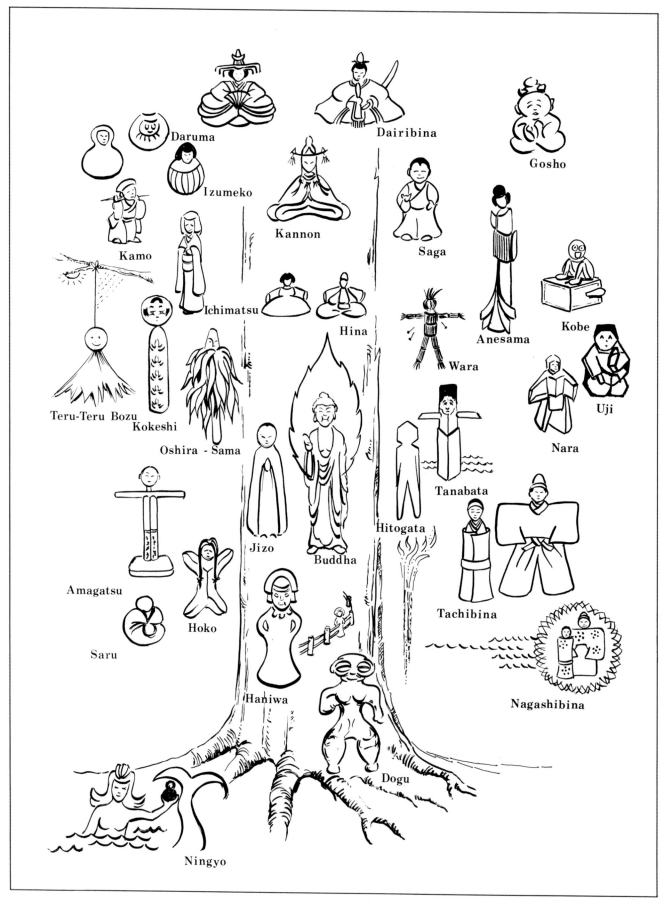

Identification Chart and Line Drawing

The identification charts and line drawings are meant to furnish general information about the most—and least—current dolls of Japan. The Dogū and Haniwa figures, like the Buddhist statuary are not, in the accepted sense of the word, dolls. They have been included because they are at the root of the 'image' tradition; that they exercised influence on the later development of various shapes and techniques is evident. Dolls mentioned in the text, but not further illustrated, are shown as small drawings: Nagashibina, Amagatsu, Hitogata, Tanabatabina, and Oshira-sama, so that readers may see what these dolls actually looked like. The mermaid is, of course, 'une petite fantaisie'. Indications of size, dates and materials are approximate, no two dolls are ever exactly alike. There are always exceptions which confirm the rule—the giants and the mini-sizes, the Kamo and Costume dolls with ivory heads and hands, wooden Tachibina decorated in the Saga manner, depicting Yoshitsune and Benkei with Jirozaemon heads! In the past as now, individual artisans used artistic licence to experiment and express personal taste. Artists and craftsmen carved Buddhist images, statues, dolls, and *netsuke*, as well as domestic furniture. It is undoubtedly due to their versatility and skill that we owe the amazing diversity of shapes, sizes and techniques.

	DOGŪ	HANIWA	HOKO	TACHIBINA (Always Pair)
Size	About 35 cm	30–150 cm	10–35 cm	Male: 10–25 cm Female: 5–20 cm
First made circa	5,000 B.C. Jōmon period	A.D. 250–552 Tumulus period	14th–15th century	Late 15th century
Material used	Baked clay.	Baked clay.	Silk, stuffing, wood, human and thread hair.	Paper: gold, plain, painted, and patterned. Thin textiles over paper. Round heads: old and Jirozaemon type. Oval heads: later date.
Technique	Hand formed.	Hand formed and moulded.	Stuffed silk body, wooden head, and painted features.	Cut, folded and glued. Head inserted. Wood and *gofun* covered. Very finely painted features.
Characteristics	Round and owl-shaped faces. Goggle eyes.	Hollow. Eyes and mouths perforated.	X-shaped body, moon face and long hair.	Female always smaller than male (reaches to shoulders). Top of male's costume matches female's dress.

	GOSHO	NARA	UJI	KAMO
Size	5–100 cm	5–25 cm	5–8 cm	2–10 cm
First made circa	Early 17th century	17th century	17th century	18th century
Material used	Baked clay. Sculptured paulownia wood. Pulverized wood and binding agent.	Wood (cypress)	Wood (tea bush)	Wood (willow)
Technique	Hand formed and moulded. *Gofun* covered and painted. Features modelled and painted.	*Ittōbori*: one knife carving. Bright colours.	*Ittōbori*: one knife carving. Soft colours.	*Kimekomi*: wood incised and crêpe and brocade pushed tightly into incisions.
Characteristics	Clothes none or minimal. Large head, white skin. Some have clothes and hair. Subject: baby boys.	Sharp, angular planes. Subject: Noh actors.	Small size. Subject: woman tea picker. Rustic.	Small size. Faces left in natural colour.

	SAGA	DARUMA	KOKESHI	IZUMEKO
Size	6–25 cm	5–100 cm	5–100 cm	2–20 cm
First made circa	18th century	——	18th to early 19th century	——
Material used	Wood	Papier-mâché and various others.	Various woods.	Various.
Technique	Relief gesso. Colours and gold.	Formed on a wooden model, cut, glued together, weighted and painted.	Lathe turned sphere and cylinder.	Various. Mostly *kimekomi*.
Characteristics	Refined execution. Some have movable heads and tongues.	Tumbler or roly-poly doll. Red and gold.	Always female. Painted decoration and shape characteristic for each production centre.	Subject: children in baskets. Base rounded in basket form.

	ICHIMATSU	TAKEDA, Festival and Costume dolls	ANESAMA	KOBE
Size	15–50 cm	10–75 cm	10–30 cm	6–8 cm
First made circa	Mid 18th century.	Takeda: late 18th–early 19th century. Doll festival: end 16th century. Fixed date: 3rd March circa 1685.	Paper dolls have been made since the 8th century.	End 19th century to early 20th century.
Material used	Head: sawdust, glue, *gofun*, encrusted glass eyes. Hair: human, silk. Body: papier-mâché, stuffed or wood. Textile joints.	Head: wood or sawdust and glue, *gofun* covered. Eyes: glass or painted. Body: rice straw or rushes. Hands and feet: carved wood, *gofun* covered or painted.	Paper: plain (*irogami*), patterned (*chiyogami*) and small accessories.	Wood, ebony, bone. Mechanism.
Technique	Limbs joined to body with textile joints.	Head on pointed stick or metal pin inserted in straw body. Clothes padded, embroidered and glued. Wig or implanted hair.	Folded and shaped by hand.	Hand carved, rustic.
Characteristics	Real clothes and accessories. Hair female: human, silk. Hair male: painted.	Takeda: exaggerated and mannered poses and expressions. Edo festival and costume dolls have personality, but later examples are stereotype.	Tall, slim figures. No facial features.	Negroid type. Torso and head on box with mechanism. Mostly black colour.

PART I
The IMAGE

HANIWA

Probably these distinctive figures evolved from the simple clay cylinders placed round the burial mounds as earth retainers or spirit fences, separating the land of the dead from that of the living. Originally they were cylinders joined by a transversal bar and punctuated at short distances by figurines of humans and animals. The word circle (*hani*=clay, *wa*=circle) can be used to denote that the clay figures were placed in circles, had circular bases or were cylindrical in shape. It is a fact that the circle has always had a deep magical meaning for primitive man the world over. It is the sign of the unchanging cycle of the seasons of nature and the seasons of life, the symbol of sun and moon, givers of light and fecundity.

Some historians substitute these figurines for human sacrifices as in China and Egypt, but to this day no conclusive evidence has been discovered in support of this theory. The term *junshi* 'following in death' makes no distinction between voluntary death and human sacrifice. Although in the *Nihongi*, also called *Nihon-shoki* in Japan, it is said that the Emperor Suinin (died c. A.D. 70), taking pity on the lamenting victims buried alive up to their shoulders around the tomb of Prince Yamato-Hiko no Mikoto, his younger brother (died c. 2 BC) formally forbade the practice and ordered clay figurines to be made instead. The *Nihongi* gives a realistic account of the burial "Yamato-Hiko was buried at Tsukizaka in Musa. Thereupon his personal attendants were assembled, and were all buried alive upright in the precinct of the tomb. For several days they died not, but wept and wailed day and night. At last they died and rotted. Dogs and crows gathered and ate them."

When the Empress, Hibasu-Hime no Mikoto died c. A.D. 3., Emperor Suinin's minister, Nomi no Sukune, summoned a hundred clay workers from the Land of Izumo and directed them to make "shapes of men, horses, and various objects, which he presented to the Emperor, saying:—Henceforward let it be the law for future ages to substitute things of clay for living men, and to set them up at tumuli." So the things of clay were first set up at the tomb of Hibasu-Hime no Mikoto. They were called Haniwa (clay rings) or Tatemono (things set up).

The *Kojiki* and *Nihongi* are the oldest written records of Japanese history (eighth century). They show much Chinese influence and include mythological accounts of the origin of the Japanese people and the divine descendance of the first Japanese Emperor from the Sun goddess, Amaterasu. Although the accounts provide precious information, some is evidently fictitious and given dates are far from accurate.

It is also possible that ritual suicide was committed by grieving next of kin and faithful servants, a custom not limited to Japan, and followed as late as 1912 by General Nogi and his wife at the death of the Meiji

Emperor, Mutsuhito.

Possibly the stauettes symbolize continued service to the deceased in the other world, but one prefers to think of them as rich gifts, destined to make the hereafter as happy as possible for the departed spirits, to placate them and stop them returning to this world to haunt the living. Haniwa figures were made in great numbers until the Buddhist religion came to Japan in the 6th century; cremation became a current practice and clay figurines were no longer needed.

The hollow figures (ranging in size from 30 to 150 cm) are simply and unpretentiously made, without superfluous decoration—the open mouths and eyes, the suspended movement, the melancholic and mysterious atmosphere emanating from them, place them among the most distinctive and outstanding examples of funerary art in the world. They contain three basic elements; earth, water and fire—the very essence of all life in a petrified phase. The birth of the human image and its meaning in Japanese art.

KANNON

Buddhism had existed for more than a thousand years before it reached Japan. It had probably been unofficially known since cultural contacts with Korea had been established in the first century. Officially it was the presentation of ritual objects and a statue of Buddha by Syong-Myong, the Korean King of Paekche (Kudara) to the Japanese emperor Kimmei that introduced Buddhism to Japan.

It had travelled a long and glorious road. From its birthplace in Nepal, along the silk routes of Central Asia, it moved across India, crossed Tibet, China and Korea before arriving in Japan in approximately A.D. 552. It penetrated Burma, Thailand and Sri Lanka, leaving in its wake marvels of architecture, sculpture and painting. Its missionaries had a humanizing and civilizing effect, for they travelled far and wide, taking with them material as well as spiritual betterment.

Buddhism was a peaceable religion, utterly devoid of violence (a force), characterized by its ready adaption and assimilation of other religious cults and their gods. It was, without any doubt, the religion which had the most powerful and far-reaching influence on all aspects of Asian art.

There was a short clash between the Soga clan which favoured Buddhism, and the conservative Mononobe clan, which opposed it on the grounds that it would counter Shinto. Shinto "the Way of the Gods", was the indigenous belief of Japan. It deified the spirits of nature, emperors and heroes, with the accent on ritual purity. It was sober with a minimal iconography. The Mahayana or "Greater Vehicle Buddhism" with its host of heavenly beings and manifestations of Buddhas and boddhisattvas ever ready to aid humanity, appealed greatly to the masses. In less than 50 years it was firmly established throughout the country.

The greatest protector and promotor of the new faith was the Prince Regent Shotoku Taishi. During his reign many temples and monasteries were founded, principally with the aid of Korean monks, nuns and architects. Early Buddhist art in Japan is for the major part indebted to China and Korea. Two of the most splendid figures of Kannon, the Guze Kannon and the Kudara Kannon (Asuka period 552–646, Horyu-ji, Nara) are said to have been made in Korea or by Korean sculptors working in Japan.

Kannon is the Japanese form of Avalokitesvara, originally of male gender in India. Popularly known as "Goddess of Mercy" in Japan, although not showing any pronounced female characteristics, the face is perhaps the most womanly among Buddhist statuary. (The British Museum possesses an exceptional *netsuke* showing an indubitably feminine Kannon suckling a puppy. Mercy extends to all living beings; the dog is also symbolic of an easy childbirth.) The gentle Jizo and the merciful Kannon are the most popular and revered deities of the Buddhist pantheon. Kannon has six major manifestations (the Roku Kannon of Tendai Buddhism) and 33 minor ones. The cult spread swiftly when places of pilgrimage were established over the entire country (Sanjusankasho) in series of 33, one for each of Kannon's manifestations. Kannon promises salvation to the faithful who visit all these temples in turn.

Kannon is implored for spiritual and material assistance, and possesses the power to purify, heal, vanquish evil and to grant power and riches to mankind. It is therefore not surprising that Kannon is sometimes represented with eleven faces in the headdress (*juichimen*) and two to a thousand arms. The two magnificent Nara-period statues, the sitting Senju (thousand-armed) Kannon in the Fujii-dera and the standing Senju Kannon in the Toshodai-ji (both in Nara) have their thousand arms forming haloes around them. By sheer golden splendour and their impressive number, the 1001 Kannons of Sanjusangendo (Hall of Thirty-three Bays) in Kyoto (1266), leave an unforgettable impression of radiance and glory. These many-headed-and-armed deities are certainly inspired by esoteric Indian and Tibetan images and symbolize the omnipotent and all-seeing emanations of Buddha.

An extremely rare representation of Kannon shows the deity as the giver of children, the life force personified. It is a simple figure radiating peace and strength, a small child on its lap wrapped in the folds of the robe. The face with the inlaid cristal eyes has a calm, introspective gaze. The figure is broadly and strongly constructed to contrast with the weak, helpless child. The impression of majesty and protectiveness

is well-portrayed. The artist has not expressed a personal vision but rendered a religious concept (divine power, fecundity) as accurately as possible. In this purpose he has admirably succeeded with convincing simplicity.

Note: Materials used for religious statues
   Wood: Mostly Japanese cypress

   Exceptionally: { Sandalwood
                    Camphor wood
                    Paulownia wood

   Finishes: { Coloured lacquer
               Gold lacquer
               Paint
               Gold leaf

   Execution: { 1. single piece-*ichibokucho*
                2. separately carved
                   pieces assembled *-yosegizukuri*

   Bronze: Casting and lost wax process
           Chasing and embossing

   Stucco: Wooden frame, wire for details (fingers, etc)
           Wrapped straw or flax
           Plastered with rough, then fine mud
           Finished with fine mud and mica mixture
           Painted
           Method imported from T'ang China (rare!)

   Dry lacquer (*kanshitsu*):
           1. Lacquer and flax applied to clay base
              when formed and dry the clay core is removed
           2. Wooden core, finely sculpted, left inside the image

   Stone: Rare inside temples—many in villages and outskirts,
          in temple gardens, along roads, on graves

A unique and rare tendency during the Kamakura period was the production of nude or semi-nude statues, meant to be dressed in textile robes donated by worshippers.

JIZO

The gentle Jizo—his Sanskrit name is Ksitigarbha or womb of the earth—who came to Japan from India via China like many other Buddhist deities, is now more revered and loved in Japan than in his country of origin. He is a boddhisattva or Buddhist saint, who compassionately renounced eternal bliss until all humanity reaches salvation. He is usually depicted as a shaven mendicant monk, carrying the *shakujo*, a sistrum or staff with loose rings, with which he forces open the gates of hell and the precious *tama*, a pearl that lights up the darkness. He is the patron saint of pregnant women, travellers and children. His image, carved in stone, weathered and moss-covered, crumbling or triumphant, has stood for centuries in the towns and villages of Japan. He is essentially the god of the people, the humble villagers, the simple countryfolk who could not commission famous artists to make bronze, wood or lacquer images. He is made of stone, hewn from the living volcanic Japanese rock, one with the earth on which the Japanese farmers live, work and die.

At crossroads and on gravestones he protects mankind in this world and the next, as his greatest power is to save the suffering souls in hell. One of the most touching and unusual images is found on a damaged tombstone in the temple garden of a Tokyo suburb, where incendiary bombs fell during World War II. The body of the standing Jizo has totally disappeared, leaving a white silhouette on the background; his serene face is left, and his arms are still tenderly holding a small child and its doll. It is not unusual to see Jizo with articles of baby clothing, food, drink, dolls and toys at his feet and he is often honoured and thanked with gifts of red caps and bibs.

According to Buddhist lore, after death the souls of little children must go to *sai-no-kawara*, a dried-up riverbed in Hell. There, a cruel old witch, Shozuka Baba and her demon horde steal their clothes and force them to build towers to Heaven with heaps of stones, but regularly destroy their work, so that they will never reach their destination.

With infinite compassion Jizo consoles the sad and tired little babes, helps them to build their towers, or hides the smallest ones in his long sleeves and takes them to Paradise. Stones placed on the head, shoulders and feet of an image, symbolize prayers and aid for dead children.

He also helps animals, for an animal can be a reincarnation of a human being. It is for this reason that the Buddhist religion forbids the killing and eating of animals. He has admirable names—The Eternal Guardian, He who embraces human nature, The Radiant King. He has many functions in aid of suffering humanity, bringing rain when needed, putting out fires, stopping earthquakes and finding thieves. Jizo is never treated humourously or irreverently by Japanese artists, the simply rendered facial expression reflects only the deep inner peace and serenity of one who knows everything about human nature with all its virtues and vices, has accepted it as such and will never stop loving and helping travellers through a fleeting world of illusion.

Note: There are some points of comparison between Jizo, Daruma and the Taoist sennin, Kaku-Dai-Tsu, who allowed children to build a tower of stones on his head while meditating on the bank of a dry river and continued his meditation for six years, without moving. The pyramid of stones remained on his head intact.

The belief that clothes could be stolen from the dead also existed in the Philippines (Ifugao). A hole was burned in each garment worn by the dead before burial "so that the spirit Ibwa would not be tempted to steal them".

DARUMA

Who does not know him, the most lovable and popular roly-poly in the Japanese isles? His official title is Bodhidharma or Law of Enlightenment and his familiar name is *okiagari koboshi*, the little monk who gets up easily. To be found wherever dolls, toys and souvenirs are sold—also at the first temple festival of the year where he is bought as an *engi*, a religious or luck-bringing object. The Daruma-ichi or fair of Gumma Prefecture is the most famous. When you buy a Daruma, you buy hope and courage, for if you have a wish to make or a feat to accomplish, you must paint one eye and promise to paint the other when your wish is granted and your dream comes true. Even if this does not help, he still gives a lesson in perseverance, for if you push him down, he will always return to the upright position, meaning 'try again'; a reminder of priest Ganjin's six attempts to reach Japan.

The classic Daruma is made of *hariko* or papier-mâché: paper softened with rice-paste is put round a roughly carved wooden model, when the paper is dry, it is cut in two parts and taken from the core. The two halves are then glued together, weighted at the base and painted red, white and gold. Common, too, is the small wooden one with fortune-telling papers inside, a blend of religion and superstition. An old Daruma is never thrown away, but taken to a local temple where he is honourably cremated on a funeral pyre.

It is interesting to look somewhat deeper into the history of the unassuming toy image and to trace its origin back to the venerable monk. Daruma is a transliteration of the Sanskrit word Dharma or Law. He was the son of a minor Indian king, the twenty-eighth Zen patriarch. He went to China in the sixth century to propagate the Dhyana, Ch'an or Zen Buddhism. There, facing a wall, he meditated for nine years without moving or speaking to achieve *satori* or illumination and his legs withered away. By some miracle—some say a painter, believing him to be an antique statue, was going to renovate him with a coat of paint—he recovered the use of his legs and is thereafter depicted defying every law of gravity by crossing the Sea of Japan (although the Chinese are certain it was the Yangtze) standing on a reed or a bamboo leaf. That is the stuff of miracles! He worked with zeal and devotion for Zen Buddhism became more popular in Japan than in China, especially among the warrior class and the literati, who found the simplicity and austerity of Zen more fitting to their lives. He also had an extraordinarily long life, having arrived in China in AD 520 and in Japan in AD 813! This, however, is no absolute record as the biblical Methuselah is stated to have lived 969 years.

Daruma is credited with the introduction of tea to China and Japan. He fell asleep while meditating and was so angry at his lapse, that he cut off his eye-lids: where he threw them the tea-bush took root. A wonderful legend indeed! Tea was then drunk by the Buddhist monks to keep them awake during meditation. Green tea was also attributed medicinal virtues and became a national beverage. It is likely that in the course of history this legend derived from the story of Priest Ganjin, a Chinese monk who lost his eyesight during his six attempts to reach Japan (753). Historically it was the priest Eisai or Yosai who introduced the Rinzai teachings of Zen Buddhism from China in 1191, who also brought the use of *matcha* or finely powdered green tea to the Japanese monasteries. The tea ordinarily used was brick tea, a dried paste made of pounded tea leaves, mentioned in Heian period cronicles (794–1185). Another source states that tea-tasting parties were held by the elegant society of the Yoshino period (1224–1392), near a Buddhist painting or statue to commemorate the introduction of tea from T'ang China by the Buddhist saints Saicho and Kukai (Kobo Daishi) at the turn of the eighth and ninth centuries. It is evident that we may take our 'pick' of tea . . . . .

It is a fact that many religious, cultural and agricultural exchanges took place by the intermediary of Buddhist monks travelling between China and Japan and that from the thirteenth century on, there was a monastic custom of communal tea-drinking before an image of the Zen patriarch. This custom also gave rise to the tea-ceremony.

Daruma is seldom taken seriously by Japanese artists. (It all began when he meditated for nine years—how can a Japanese take 'au sérieux' someone who sits still for nine solid years?) Many representations of Daruma seem to be more of a caricature than of a portrait, the only constant factors being the red robe of an Indian monk, the fly-whisk (*hossu*) and the fierce eyes. He is shown covered with cobwebs, stretching and yawning most rudely, with a disproportionally large mouth, walking happily with a courtesan with whom he has exchanged clothes—illumination is accessible to all—or even with an erotic or *shunga* book! There are many variant and regional Darumas made in Japan. Niigata has the *sankaku* or triangular Daruma inspired by the straw head-to-knees rain- and snowcoats of the peasants, Ishikawa produces a solid lacquer one—the prefecture has a flourishing lacquer industry, it also makes a red and white pair in papier-mâché. Matsuyama has an *onna* or woman Daruma with real hair, the lady Daruma from Oita is the plainest of the family. Okame, the goddess of mirth is sometimes depicted in *netsuke* art disguised as a woman Daruma, but when turned upside down it becomes apparent that she is not as demure as she looks. Onna Daruma is a joke on the gentle sex being unable to sit still without speaking for any length of time, and when children make a snowman they call him Yuki (snow) Daruma. Apart from the humorous aspects, many artists were inspired by this intriguing personality to produce masterpieces of *netsuke* art, *zenga* or *zen* painting, ceramic and wooden images.

The Japanese say he was buried on Mount Kataoka. The Chinese say he was buried in their country but was seen travelling back to India three years after his death carrying one sandal. When his tomb was opened, only a sandal was found. Bodhidharma, the first Chinese Zen patriarch, had returned to the country where truth and legend live side by side . . . .

The representation (page 57) is of a Tibetan Tantric bronze of a dhyana boddhisattva or emanation of Buddha, named Avalokitesvara-Sadaksari (Dharma). He was the guardian deity of the Land of Snow (Tibet) and the Dalai Lama was his reincarnation on earth. The god has four arms and is seated in dhyanasana or pose of meditation. A pair of hands is joined in the gesture of homage and adoration, the raised right hand holds the rosary with 108 beads, the left, the lotus with eight petals. The picture shows how Indian stylistic influences were transmitted by Nepalese artists to Southern Tibet and from there to China and Japan resulting in unrecognizable extremes. The photo bears witness to other possible transfigurations of religious concepts and iconography.

Note: Daruma is a pronounced case of dual personality; he can be ascetic or lecherous, fierce or gentle, fanatic or feeble, comical or awe-inspiring, ridiculous or noble—in short, perfectly human.

Dharma.

ZEN

For a doctrine which cannot be explained in words or writing, much has been said and written about Zen. Perhaps the best explanation lies in the words of the French writer Antoine de Saint-Exupéry: 'Ferme les yeux, on ne voit bien qu'avec le coeur'—'Close your eyes, one only sees well with the heart'. In the East it is said to be a sudden, instinctive illumination of the spirit, after years of a tranquil, inward directed scrutiny. The Buddha himself failed to attain enlightenment after fasting almost to the point of death. With illumination comes the understanding that every existing person and thing is part of and in harmony with the Buddha-nature and that all deeds should be done as perfectly and naturally as possible. The Buddha-nature is present in a molehill and a mountain, a courtesan and a saint. The piece of wood is Buddha and Buddha is the piece of wood and both are part of the Buddha-nature. In the wood one can see a tree growing from seed to giant in all the beauty of its living force. One can simply hear the wind in its branches or the music of Vivaldi's 'Four Seasons'. It is all Buddha-nature.

'Once there was a small seed. It met with favourable conditions and the life it carried awakened and it grew. It put out roots to search for food and stretched its head to find the light. It rained, it snowed and sometimes it was very hot. The seed became a tree. The tree grew tall and strong. The tree was powerful; and the elements could not break it. The birds built their nests among the sheltering branches and found a safe resting place for their weary wings and sang their songs high and clear. The tree gave beauty when it flowered, shade when it was hot and fruit when its leaves turned to gold. The tree did this because it was in its nature to give only joy. One day when the tree had reached maturity, it was cut down in all its splendour—and still it gave—from its wood men made houses and temples, sculptures and toys, crutches and bridges and firewood. One little piece became Buddha, and the soul of the tree was Buddha and all that the tree had been. From seed to growing tree, from wood to sculpture we experience the cycle of life and death and rebirth. When we look at a rough piece of wood sculptured by nature and the figure of Buddha sculptured by a human hand, we experience Buddha-nature, man and nature in perfect harmony.'

GOSHO

The Gosho doll is of noble descent, the name means 'palace doll' and it originated in the Kyoto Imperial palace. When the Tokugawa Shoguns were in power, and had established their new military capital, Edo, the 'sankin kotai' or alternative attendance, came into being. By this law, powerful lords were required to pay ceremonial (and expensive) visits to Edo, every other year, while their wives and children stayed there permanently as hostages. This drained their funds and ruled out plots against the Shogun. On their journey along the Tokaido road, they also visited the Imperial Palace in Kyoto, and the Gosho doll was the token gift in exchange for their tribute.

The oldest kinds were made of clay covered with a layer of *gofun*, but later the best examples were carved from kiriwood (Paulownia imperialis), also covered with a coat of *gofun*. *Gofun* is a paste made of glue, aleuron and powdered oyster shell, which gives an absolutely smooth and shiny finish when dried and polished with the tokusa plant—an efficient polish, because the white hare living on the moon, is said to rub its home with it! The features were delicately painted with a cat's hair brush. Cat's hair has the advantages of being very flexible and holding paint well, because it is thicker at the tip than at the base.

Although some dolls have clothes and hair, in most examples the clothing is limited to a strict minimum and is either painted or pasted on; by tradition they represent chubby, almost naked, vigorous little boys of five years of age with white skin and a disproportionally large head. Many subjects, real and legendary are represented and are cases of "*mitate*" or substitution: although they are babies, they have the attributes of national heroes, sumo wrestlers, the seven lucky gods, well-known dances—the repertory is so varied that a pocket history of Japan could be compiled by tracing the origins of these miniature personages.

The Gosho doll was not a plaything but essentially a presentation doll. As it represented a baby boy, it was a wish for strong and healthy male offspring, and also a wish for a safe trip, some dolls carrying a talisman on their backs to ward off evil spirits. Ladies of the court and imperial concubines kept them as fertility charms. For the Emperor and those in power, it was a necessity to have a male successor, so for them good fortune began with healthy male children. The Gosho doll was known by different names, allowing it to be easily recognized, such as—*shirajishi ningyō* or white skinned doll; *zudai ningyō* or big headed doll.

Gosho dolls, originally the privilege of the aristocracy, gradually became widely popular among the inhabitants of the big cities. They were not 'pretty' dolls, but showed originality and a character which place them in a special category. T. Kitamura cites a famous dollmaker of Osaka, Izukura. His 'Gosho' dolls were known as Izukura *ningyō*.

Sizes ranged from 3 cm to 1 m. In the Genroku period (1688–1704), under the Shogun Yoshimune, there was such display of wealth that sumptuary laws were promulgated; they regulated every detail of daily life, down to the size of children's dolls, which were not to exceed 20 cm.

NARA AND NOH

Nara dolls originated at a famous shrine, namely the Kasuga shrine built by Fujiwara Fuhito to the memory of his ancestors in 710. It is one of the oldest and most venerable shrines of Japan, well-known for its great number of stone and bronze lanterns and herds of tame deer. The deer is looked upon as the messenger of the gods (*kami-no-tsukai*) and thus a sacred animal.

Nara having been the capital (645–794) before Kyoto conserves many ancient traditions kept alive by festivals which include music (Gagaku), dance (Bugaku and Dengaku), mime, posturing and magic (Sarugaku), and plays (Noh and Kyogen). Kyogen is the comic interlude between the different acts of a Noh play. Bugaku was introduced from China in the eighth century. Originally the pastime of the aristocracy who performed the dances in their palaces and in temples on state occasions; Bugaku=court dances. Dengaku was a religious pantomime accompanied by songs, performed by itinerant priests. It derived from a peasant dance which was popular in the seventh and eighth centuries and included elements of the ritual praying for peace and abundant harvests; Dengaku=dance of the rice fields. Because Nara dolls almost invariably represent Noh actors, and because the earliest Noh plays were religious in context and performed at shrines, there is definitely a link between the magic ritual and the officiating priest, which later became the play and the actor.

Shinto is an animistic religion. Rituals to placate and petition the *kami*, divinities, spirits present in nature, were held at shrines. They were also used to educate illiterate people and show them that their survival depended on natural forces; 'the hostile gods, let us try to be friends with them, the powers that cause death, illness and famine, let us appease them by gifts, by music, by dances and chants, rituals and amulets, even by cheating them and wearing masks and giving them images representing us'. Man versus the gods of nature; man forever fighting, man winning by his reasoning power the battle against superstition and the unmeasurable strength of the elements.

From this magic ritual, the interchanging and blending of Dengaku and Sarugaku, Noh theatre developed into the greatest art form of the Muromachi period. Zeami was the leading figure in its evolution and it was to become the favourite pastime of the literati and the *samurai*.

It was a theatre of subtle suggestion rather than direct statement. The mask and stiff, sumptuous robe identified the personage. His fan was his most important accessory in the stylized posturing, indicating the type of play and the character being portrayed. It could also represent other objects. Every gesture, word, and movement had a meaning. For the actor it is a play of non-identity, his face hidden by the mask, his body by the clothes. His genius lies in being the invisible mechanism, which gives life to a lifeless mask and a magnificent costume. The only stage decor, an old, gnarled pinetree, is another indication of the animistic origin of Noh: spirits live in very old trees.

And so we come to the first Nara dolls, small, wooden Noh figures decorating the hats of priests and musicians at the Kasuga shrine festival. They were executed in a technique called *ittō-bori* meaning 'one knife carving', cut in sharp, angular planes and painted in strong, pure colours. The material used was invariably cypress wood. Okano Heiemon originated the Nara doll in the seventeenth century and the tradition was carried on by the Okano family for thirteen generations. Were these little figures adapted and used as *netsuke* or did some imaginative carver find his inspiration in them?

Ueda Reikichi tells us that quite a number of Uji and Nara dollmakers also carved *netsuke*, the most famous, the paragon, being Morikawa Toen-'At seventeen he began to study Noh comedy (Kyogen) in the school of Yamada Hachiemon and mastered it. In March 1854 the Emperor attended a play in which Toen acted. He was the paragon of the great mastercarvers of Nara *ningyō* (1820–1894)'. Toen had numerous imitators, but not many of the rare little figures that can definitely be attributed to him have survived. They are much coveted by *netsuke* and doll collector alike.

Although Noh is difficult to understand, its primary purpose is to awaken in the spectator a pure, aesthetic experience, named *yūgen*. The great Zeami described *yūgen* as "crystal snow in a silver chalice"—but the most beautiful and apt description comes from Bernard Leach, who saw it as a "ghostly flowering".

KAMO

During the Heian period the capital of Japan was Kyoto or Heiankyo, 'the Citadel of Peace and Tranquillity'; built on the same architectural plan as the Chinese capital Chang-an, it remained the Imperial capital until the Meiji era. There a puppet Emperor lived, submerged in a sea of vain intrigues, endless ceremonies, and prescribed aesthetics, while real power was wielded by the powerful Fujiwara clan. It was, however, a time when all art forms flourished and were greatly encouraged.

Two precious literary sources of information and historical importance are "*The Tale of Genji*" (Genji Monogatari) by Murasaki Shikibu (born 978) and "*The Pillow Book*" (Makura-no-soshi) by Sei Shonagon (born 965). These two world famous literary achievements were made possible by the emergence of the *kana* syllabary, the indigenous script of Japan. Both writers were ladies-in-waiting at the Imperial Court and in their books we find mention of playthings and a dolls' house. Murasaki Shikibu, in chapter 7, The Festival of Maples, describes the dolls' house used, alas, to seduce young Violet on long term! Kyoto National Museum possesses album leaves of the Tosa school, one painting shows the child Violet admiring a dolls' house filled with dolls dressed and coiffed in Heian style.

The worldly Sei Shonagon is more sensitive to the beauty and pathos of things (*mono-no-aware*), and in her list of 'Things that Arouse a Fond Memory of the Past' are included: dried hollyhock, a night with a clear moon, last year's paper fan, an old love letter and . . . the objects used during the Display of Dolls. (Hiina Asobi=Display of Dolls). And again, in her list of 'Adorable Things': "the face of a child drawn on a melon, the objects used during the Display of Dolls . . . . One picks up a tiny lotus leaf that is floating on a pond and examines it. Not only lotus leaves, but little hollyhock flowers, and indeed all small things are most adorable. Duck eggs. An urn containing the relics of some holy person. Wild pinks . . . ." She was also a most eclectic collector.

There were two festivals at the Kamo shrine; the main Shinto celebration of the year, which was observed in the middle of the fourth month and a 'special' festival, also held annually since the end of the ninth century at the end of the eleventh month. Two days before its opening there was a formal rehearsal of dance and music in front of the Imperial or Seiryo Palace. On the day of the festival the groups proceeded from the palace to the shrine where the performance was carried out, they then returned to the palace and performed an encore: the Sacred Dance of the Return.

Kamo dolls were originally made in the first half of the eighteenth century at the Kamo Shrine by priests or craftsmen in the service of the shrine, to be sold as souvenirs and charms. Their development is ascribed to one Takahashi Tadashige, who made the dolls from leftover pieces of the willow wood and scraps of brocade and silk, used for the shrine festival. They are, in fact, small wooden statues of which head, hands and feet are carved and left in the natural wood colour, the features delicately painted. The body is then clothed by a technique called *kimekomi*, loosely translated meaning 'push (textile) into wood to form a pattern'. The contours of the clothing are deeply incised in the wooden figure and then covered with different kinds of textiles, which are lightly glued and tightly pushed into the cuts, thus forming the different layers and designs of the clothes.

Nearly all Kamo dolls have four points in common: their small size (3 to 10 cm), their smiling faces (showing that they are in a festive mood), their triangular mouth, which accentuates their friendliness, and the orange crêpe and green brocade used for their costumes. Orange and green textiles are much used for the older dolls of many types, can it be that these vegetable and mineral dyes were easiest to obtain or were they more resistant to fading? The green dye is prepared from the indigo plant (genus Indigofera). The orange dye is made from safflower heads (Carthamus tinctorius).

Contemporary dolls are no longer called Kamo but *kimekomi*, after the technique. They are usually bigger, more colourful, more static than the originals and have *gofun*-covered heads, hands and feet. The basic figure is made of pulverized Paulownia wood and a binding agent such as glue or lacquer. There are dollmaking schools teaching the *kimekomi* method, and shops selling the materials for nimble fingers. It is to be noted that real Kamo dolls are all wood, with clothes made by the *kimekomi* technique, that they are extremely rare and only to be found in private collections and museums such as the Kyoto National Museum which has a representative collection of these dolls, as well as of many other kinds.

SAGA

The name Saga is misleading, for the dolls did not originate in Saga Prefecture in Western Kyushu, but in Saga, a small town near Kyoto. They have the privilege of being the rarest and most mysterious personages among the dolls of Japan. Most sources agree that they were made in the early eighteenth century by Buddhist monks or temple craftsmen, who were also sculptors of Buddhist figures (*busshi*). Another theory is that they were created by the artisans who made Noh masks (the *men-uchi*): they were also eminent carvers and were skilled in the use of *gesso* or *sabi* a mixture of whetstone powder, water and lacquer.

Saga dolls were true decorative statuettes and crafted and finished to a high degree. The basic figure was made of carved wood, to which a layer of *gesso* was applied. It was then decorated. The colour palette is typical: rich, dark hues of red, brown, black, and beige, given depth by a generous use of gold. The relief work and ornamental gilding of the clothes, show a marked resemblance to the decoration found on the robes of Buddhist statues. Many Saga *ningyō* represent young temple attendants (Doji) carrying small animals such as dogs, birds, and roosters. Basil Hall Chamberlain, translator of the 'Kojiki', tells us that an indigenous Japanese term for Buddha was Hotoke. Hotei, one of the seven lucky gods of Japan, is sometimes referred to as 'the happy Buddha'. A statue of the god Hotei, executed in the Saga manner, is to be found at the Manpuku-ji in Uji, perhaps constituting additional proof of the religious origin of Saga dolls.

Some Saga dolls are in a decidedly playful mood, and shake their heads and put out tongues when moved (*kubifuri*). By this mechanism they resemble the European porcelain 'nabots', dwarfs and exotic figurines made in France and Germany in the eighteenth century, with mobile heads, arms and legs. They were so-called 'chinoiseries', European interpretations of Asian subjects.

Because of their growing popularity, a shop making and selling Saga style dolls, was opened in Edo in the late eighteenth century. These dolls, however, were more colourful and dynamic than the originals. Although well-made, they seem to miss the strength of structure and feeling of quiet refinement, the muted, deep colouring of the true Saga doll, the nobility of manner, which distinguishes the aristocrat from the imposter.

KOKESHI

The Kokeshi doll is the doll reduced to its simplest expression—a cylinder with a sphere-shaped head such as children might make in plasticine if asked to make a human figure. Although Kokeshi are probably the best known among Japanese dolls, they are relatively young as dolls and collectibles.

The farmers of the Tohoku region (in north-eastern Honshu) had long been in the habit of going to one of the numerous hot springs to cure their ailments and the practice became fashionable among the townspeople during the latter part of the Edo period. The farmers who made toys for their children and later the wood craftsmen, saw a lucrative possibility in their products and sold Kokeshi dolls to the visitors of the hot spring resorts to take home as souvenirs, each prefecture having its specific type.

Perhaps Kokeshi figures were born from the folk religion practiced in Aomori and Iwate in which a god named Oshira-sama is worshipped. The image is a kind of totem, a wooden pole about one foot in height with a sculptured or drawn-on face. It is wrapped in many layers of cloth just under the face, the cloth forming a kind of cape. It was kept in the house as a protective god and possibly a phallic god, many folk images having fertility and phallic connotations in Japan. It was also used as a staff by shrine priestesses when invoking the spirits on behalf of the people.

Another possibility lies in the name itself: *ko*=child, *keshi*=erasing. In years of famine, women were unable to feed all their children and were reduced to abortion or infanticide. The new-born babes vanished so that the others should live. Kokeshi could thus have been memorial dolls, kept in the house to appease the spirits of the dead. It is a fact that the classic Kokeshi doll is always a girl, as the classic Gosho doll is always a boy. In Japan feeble girls were less wanted than strong boys. No arms, no legs—a wrapped-up child or an innocent, wistful little ghost who has no need of arms or legs? Fact can sometimes be stranger than fiction.

It is amazing how many variations on the simple sphere and cylinder-theme there are. At this time there are many kinds of decorative and commercial dolls sold in the shops, colourful souvenirs of Japan, they were born after World War II and are called 'kindai' or new type Kokeshi as opposed to 'dentō' or traditional ones; of these there are ten distinctive families, recognizable by head and body shape, facial features, colours and decoration. If the type is absolutely pure, the connoisseur and collector can immediately tell to which family the Kokeshi belongs. However, as happens in even the best families, some amount of cross-breeding has taken place, and these hybrids are not easily placed.

Two distinctive types of Kokeshi (or anti-Kokeshi) are found in Yamaguchi Prefecture, the most southerly tip of Honshu, as opposed to the prefectures of northern Honshu. One is a strange little man, having all the characteristics a classic Kokeshi doll should not have, called Kibori or Ichiboku-bori *ningyō* (single piece wood carving). The other is an elaborately lacquered, sophisticated version of the true Kokeshi doll.

The lathework is a purely mechanical process, in which a variety of inexpensive wood is used (Cornacea family and Acer pictum) but the decoration is the important part of the doll, making it a stereotype or a delicately finished and proudly signed personality, while conserving all its regional characteristics. Sizes range from a few centimeters to nearly a meter. Such dimensions are not ideal for a toy: the small ones can be accidentally swallowed or chewed, the big ones are too heavy to lift and in case of internal wars among children, the medium sized ones could inflict heavy damage! But an appealing collector's item? Definitely yes!

Note: The most plausible explanation as to the KO (child), KESHI (erasing) theory and one confirmed in Japanese stories, is the following—in earlier times, when a family was very poor and had pretty girl-children, they would be 'sold' to rich people as servants or to geisha houses for a certain sum of money. The girl was then held by contract, to return the sum plus the money spent on the acquisition of her accomplishments: musical education, poetry, dancing, and also for her clothing, food and keep, if she wished to become free. Sometimes a young girl voluntarily sold herself to ease her family's poverty, to help someone to whom she felt indebted, or to pay the doctor's bills for a loved one who was ill (Yasunari Kawabata—"*Snow Country*"). It would seem then, that the Kokeshi doll was a souvenir of a child sold into bondage, or the child's doll kept in the house as a grateful remembrance, a prayer and a plea for forgiveness. In 'Japan: An Attempt at Interpretation' (1904), Lafcadio Hearn writes that 'a father could kill or sell his children—the sale in time of extreme need, might save a house from ruin; and filial piety exacted submission to such sacrifice for the sake of the continuation of the familial ancestral cult.'

TAKEDA

What strikes the attention immediately when looking at these dolls, is their dynamism. Heads, hands and feet are set at sharp and exaggerated angles to give the impression of movement. Nearly all other dolls look static compared to them. Why is this doll so different? Takeda Ōmi I was born in the seventeenth century. He had theatrical ambitions and a good business sense, for he opened an outdoor amusement park in the suburbs of Osaka which was most imaginative for its time, and where he presented all kinds of innovative and experimental performances. Some were with live actors, some with puppets, and still others with automats (*karakuri*), earning him the nickname 'Takeda Karakuri'. These novelties were commercially rewarding and must have provided a rich and varied source of ideas for dollmakers.

The name Takeda is found more than once in accounts relating to *karakuri* (trick dolls), and the Takeda generation was surely specialized in the construction of complicated doll mechanism. A Takeda Jusaburō from Osaka is mentioned as having replaced two acrobatic *karakuri* puppets on the Fukurokuju chariot of Nagoya in 1767. The chariot's principal personage, Fukurokuju, the god of longevity, had already been made by another Takeda craftsman, Takeda Tōkichi, in the mid eighteenth century. It is doubtful that all these Takeda were directly related, as pupils were adopted, and took the name of their master or school.

In 1543 Japan established relations with the Portuguese, who brought their newest mechanical inventions, such as printing, clocks, and animated music boxes, into the country. The first clock was made by Tsuda Sukezaemon of Nagoya in 1598. It is probable that Takeda Ōmi I was inspired by these novelties, as were his descendants. There exists a *surimono* by Shunman Kubo entitled 'A rooster out of the drum'. It is a New Year's greeting card showing a Karakuri operated by Takeda Ōmi V. It is dated 1801 corresponding to the year of the rooster.

That Takeda dolls are inspired by actors and moving figures is evident in their theatrical and dynamic poses and extremely expressive, sensitively modelled and painted faces, with uptilted eyes and downturned mouths. The original stands for these dolls were very characteristically decorated in black lacquer with a cut-out decorative painted reserve called *kozama.* They look rather like a small version of the boxes on which the Karakuri dolls do their tricks and which hide the mechanism. The Takeda doll may be considered as one of the most original manifestations of the Japanese dollmaker's art. It is a doll imitating an automat, imitating a living actor!

A Short Survey of Girls' Day and Boys' Day

There are two Japanese words for doll: Ningyō and Hina (which was originally written Hiina in the Heian period), when there was a Hiina Asobi or Display of Dolls. Hiina or Hinna could be a derivation of the Sanskrit word meaning small or tiny—hence a miniature representation. Hina (which changes to *bina* in compounds) is the word most commonly used for the Girls' and Boys' Festival dolls and for general and descriptive terms.

> Tachibina = standing doll
> Suwaribina = sitting doll
> Kamibina = paper doll
> Ishōbina = costumed doll
> Tsuchibina = clay doll
> Dairibina = Imperial couple dolls
> Oshiebina = stick doll
> Kyōhobina = Kyoto doll
> Kokinbina = ancient style doll
> Sutebina = casting off doll
> Jirozaemonbina = doll made by Jirozaemon and characterized by a round head.
> Jirozaemon gashirabina = round headed doll in the style of Jirozaemon.

For Ningyō, the earliest interpretations are *katashiro* or votive figure and *hitogata* or divine shape. Ningyō (human shape), is used for most of the old dolls of a specific type and the word *ningyō* used alone extends to other playthings.

> Gosho ningyō   Nara ningyō
> Saga ningyō   Uji ningyō
> Kamo ningyō

Another meaning of the word *Ningyo* (written with a different character), is merman or mermaid. In a biography of Prince Shōtoku Taishi from the eighth century chronicles of Japan, the *'Nihongi'*, is described the following strange event: 'In the fourth month of the twenty-seventh year of Suiko, A.D. 619 (the reign of the Empress Suiko for whom the Prince acted as Regent). A merman appeared in the Gamo River in Omi (present Shiga Prefecture). The Prince's followers presented it (to him) for his inspection.'

The Soken Kisho (Appreciation of Superior Sword Furnishings), warns against dishonest merchants, who sell, at exorbitant prices, objects such as rare *netsuke* made of mermaid bone. So, a gentle warning; in Japan never mistake a mermaid for a doll!

A doll festival was instituted at the end of the Muromachi period (1338–1568) and the third day of March fixed upon about 1685. Girls' Day (Hina Matsuri), celebrated on the third day of the third month (Jomi or Sangatsu Mikka), is also known as Momo-no-Sekku, the Feast of the Peach. The peachblossom is emblematic of the feminine qualities of grace, gentleness, and of Spring. The display may consist of the Emperor and Empress pair only, or the complete set of fifteen dolls and many miniature lacquer accessories. The ancient style sets (Kokinbina) could have any number of dolls, and usually had an excessive quantity of elaborate trappings of all kinds.

The stand has five or seven tiers and is draped with a red cloth. Sometimes (but rarely), the dolls are displayed in a miniature palace. A set consists of the Emperor and Empress (*dairibina*), three ladies-in-waiting with saké implements (*kanjo*), five musicians (*gonin bayashi*): a flute player, two hand drum players, one drum player with sticks, one 'utai' or chanter with fan; two armed retainers, an old one and a young one, also named Ministers of Right (*udaijin*) and Left (*sadaijin*); three serving men or lackeys (*shicho*): two with ceremonial umbrellas and one with the Emperor's shoes. One is happy, one sad, and one is angry. These expressions are said to be due to the effect of saké!

No one has ever advanced a theory as to the event represented by all these personages. Just a court ceremony? Ueda Reikichi tells us that Shugetsu Meiwa was imprisoned for representing cherry and mandarin orange trees with his *hina* sets 'suggesting the decor of the Shishinden Hall of the Imperial Palace'. This points to a ceremony, such as an Enthronement, in the said Hall, but also to the fact that it had never been done before. Armed retainers in the imperial presence, inside the palace, seem out of place. The presence of saké pourers, ladies-in-waiting, usually dressed in the white and red robes of Shintō shrine maidens or priestesses (*miko*) indicate a marriage, as do the lacquer objects, which a lady of noble birth was obliged to bring with her as part of her dowry. Lacquered palanquins were sometimes specially made for marriages and ox-carts for Imperial processions. Yet, another possibility is ceremonial worship at the Imperial shrine. The shrine maidens, the Noh musicians (sometimes, but rarely, replaced by Gagaku musicians) indicate performances in honour of distinguished visitors. One of the lackeys holds the Emperor's shoes, considered as ritually unclean objects, showing that he is in a place to where he has travelled and that his shoes are undesirable—perhaps a Shintō shrine?

Enthronement ceremony, marriage, ritual worship, or a combination of the three? The question remains open...

Boys' Day, celebrated the fifth day of the fifth month (*gogatsu itsuka*,

Tango-no-Sekku or First Horse Day) is also known as Shōbu-no-Sekku or the Feast of the Iris. The iris has many symbolic characteristics in Japanese lore. In Heian times, two days after the dedication of the iris, the Emperor visited the Hall of Martial Arts to watch his warriors display their skill in sword-play and archery. The Kamakura period advocated the military spirit, in the best cases sublimated by Zen Buddhism. Iris leaves resemble swords and the sword was always a quasi-religious object—'the soul of the *samurai*'. On this festival day, chopped iris stalks were soaked in saké, and iris leaves put in the bath water as aids to health and longevity. Formerly people even grew iris plants on their roofs to ward off evil and used the leaves as pillows or as decoration under the eaves. Iris leaves became symbolic of swords, and swords of the military heroes of Japan. At first, *samurai* displayed their weapons outside and children played military games and waged mock battles. In the beginning of the Edo period, the arms and armour were moved inside the house and military figures were added. The display became so lavish and the figures so large, that sumptuary laws were issued. The festival was meant to encourage the spirit of *'bushido'* or Japanese chivalry—a far-reaching sense of loyalty and devotion for institutions and superiors, and the ability to overcome the difficulties and obstacles of life. Popular are the military and mythical heroes of Japanese history. The figures are arranged on a two-tiered stand covered with a green cloth. The number of military heroes is too great to be described in full, but some of the most popular personages are:

—Jimmu Tennō, the founder of the Imperial house and the first Emperor of Japan, he wears the Imperial Regalia: the mirror, jewels and sword, and carries a golden eagle on his bow.

—Shōki, the demon queller with fierce expression and bushy black beard, wearing a Chinese costume and small, horned helmet. His weapons are a halberd and a straight sword.

—The Empress Jingū (also written Jingō) and Takenouchi-no-Sukune, her minister carrying her baby son.

—Yoshitsune and Benkei (sometimes accompanied by a bannerman) in full battle armour.

—Kabuki actors performing famous historical scenes and popular dances.

—Momotarō, the Peach Boy, sometimes accompanied by a dog, monkey and pheasant.

—Kintarō, the boy Hercules of Japan, usually wrestling with a huge carp.

—Tenjin or Michizane Sugawara, the patron of learning and literature; he sits cross-legged, holds a sceptre of office (*shaku*), and wears rich court dress. There are versions with and without a long, straight, black beard. He sometimes has a plum blossom motif on his chest, in remembrance of the legend of his favourite plum tree, which uprooted itself and flew through the air, to follow him in exile.

—Fukusuke, the dwarf, unmistakable by his big head, formal dress (*kami-*

shimo) and fan. He was the most popular comic story-teller (*rakugo*) of the Edo period.

—Hotei, one of the Seven Happy Gods of Japan, with laughing face and a fat belly, he carries a rigid fan (*uchiwa*) and a full bag of treasures for (good) children.

—Katō Kiyomasa, with a typical, very high helmet, trident spear, and tiger.

—And, usually shown on horseback, Toyotomi Hideyoshi, Tokugawa Ieyasu, and, in the Meiji period, the Emperor Mutsuhito and General Nogi.

The accessories consist of helmets, arms and banners, miniature samurai armour (*kabuto ningyō*) and the white horse of the gods.

ICHIMATSU

This doll is named after a famous and handsome Kabuki actor of the eighteenth century, Sanogawa Ichimatsu of Osaka. To make a doll bearing the name of the current idol was undoubtedly a wonderful sales strategy ensuring financial success—it was also good advertising for the actor! Close to the European playdoll, it can easily be dressed and undressed because it has supple textile parts joining the limbs to the body. The oldest variation and probable ancestor is the Mitsuore or triple-jointed doll, with wooden joints at hips, knees and ankles.

The male Ichimatsu doll was rapidly given a female counterpart, who turned out to be more decorative and successful than her partner. These dolls evolved into the boy and girl dolls, representing children in their festival finery at the three-five-seven celebrations, and were perhaps given as mementos of these happy occasions. Some authors also describe these dolls as a long-sleeved *kimono* doll or Furisode *ningyō*. The long-sleeved *kimono* is still worn by little girls when they go to shrine festivals. The boys wore the formal *hakama* trousers and a *haori* coat, but this custom is no longer observed.

Both dolls had extensive wardrobes, complete down to the tiniest details: painted fans, lacquered combs and hairpins for the female doll, miniature *inro* and *netsuke* for the male: exquisite accessories made by famous artists of the day. The textiles for *kimono* and *obi* were woven, tie-dyed, painted and embroidered to scale. Today, the techniques involved in the creation of an Ichimatsu doll are much the same as those used during the eighteenth century. A mixture of sawdust and glue is moulded to form head, forearms and legs, then covered with flesh-coloured *gofun*; the face has inlaid glass eyes, which are first entirely covered and then carved out so that they reappear. Human or silk hair

is used for the distinctive, fringed hairstyle of the female. The male sometimes has painted hair, radiating in straight lines from a central point on top of the head. The features are delicately shaped and painted. Supposedly playdolls, Ichimatsu dolls are more often used as display or presentation dolls and confined to a glass case as decorative elements of the home.

As these dolls were always dressed in the traditional Japanese costume, they were also called Yamato *ningyō*—the ancient name of Japan. In 1927 there was an exchange of dolls between the children of America and Japan. The former sent more than 12000 blue-eyed dolls, about 40 cm in height; the latter reciprocated by sending 58 dolls, beautifully dressed in their festival *kimono* and as tall as six year old children. They were paid for by money collected in Japanese schools, and some are still visible in American museums. At that time they were named 'silent envoys', 'ambassadors of goodwill', and 'friendship dolls'. Another suitable title for the Ichimatsu-Furisode-Yamato doll would be the-doll-with-many-names!

The Ichimatsu doll is sometimes signed on the body by the dollmaker, but this does not permit exact dating as many generations used the same name.

Note: In the Kansai (Kyoto-Osaka) area, it was customary to give a pair of Ichimatsu dolls to young brides, symbolizing the wish for healthy boys and girls. A fact worth mentioning is that while most dolls' bodies have no visible sexual characteristics, on some they are faintly suggested, and on yet others they are explicit. Although the author has never personally seen the following phenomenon, she has read an article stating that one can find dolls purposely made with the head and clothes of girls, on male bodies, for even if the baby was a girl, it was wanted to be as strong as a boy (?). Other explanations could be a repair, or a maker with a stock of superfluous male bodies, or, knowing the far-reaching Japanese mode of allusion, a reminder of the handsome Kabuki actor, Ichimatsu; after all, Kabuki actors DO play the female roles....

TACHIBINA

Tachibina or standing dolls are thought to be the ancestors of the Dairibina or Imperial Couple. Yet another theory makes them figures for ancestor worship or the personification of the male and female principle. The term more correctly means upright dolls as they cannot stand without support. The Japanese have always been very clever in paper-making and paper-folding, so it seems logical that these dolls were made for children by older women, as an amusement for both, and to teach children respect for their ancestors and the Imperial system.

Beginning with the earliest types, Hitogata, Amagatsu, Hoko, Tachibina, and the first seated dolls, the outstretched arms are a constant factor. All the dolls before Tachibina were protectors from evil forces: Haniwa figures protected the living from the dead, paper Hitogata were bought at shrines to absorb and cure disease, then thrown in a river or burnt; wooden ones showing nailmarks exist, used for casting spells. Amagatsu made of crossed bamboo sticks, and Hoko made of stuffed white silk, protected their owners, especially children, from illness and evil spirits. Possessed children were cured by deliberately breaking a crude, painted doll, made of fired clay, sold at the Fushimi Inari Shrine in Kyoto. In every case, the outstretched arms seem to be symbolic of protection and the warding off of evil.

Another interesting feature is the difference in size and shape between the tall, broad male and the small cylindrical female doll, which is never found in other pairs. This could be a reflection of the dominating role of the male in Japanese society, or as some Japanese scholars think a transformation of the Hoko and Amagatsu dolls. They could also have been at the origin of Girls' Day, when, following an old Chinese superstition, purification rites took place on the third day of the third month (the day of the snake) and paper dolls which had been breathed on and held against the body were thrown in rivers. These dolls were called Sutebina or casting-off dolls. The wooden Tanabata doll is also an example of this custom.

Tachibina show a marked resemblance to the Nagashibina of Tottori prefecture, dating back to the fifteenth century, which are set afloat in the sea or river to take evil and illness away with them, to purify, to procure health, happiness and milk for babies. They also seem to have phallic and fertility connotations and there are two versions of these dolls—one is a man-woman pair, side by side in a round, woven straw frame—the other consists of ten pairs in a horizontal bamboo holder. Their *kimono* is usually red decorated with white plum blossoms.

Tachibina have round heads made of wood and *gofun* in the case of Jirozaemon and early types, the faces tending to become egg-shaped later. The features are minutely but delicately painted. Sometimes the heads have human or horse hair. The top of the male doll's costume matches the *kimono* of the female doll. Usually the decoration consists of flowers, auspicious symbols, geometrical and embossed designs, or even personages such as Jo and Uba, the happy old couple of Takasago. The costumes are made of painted and gold paper or paper covered with very thin textiles.

Tachibina seem to be in the majority when it comes to the doll motif as decoration of art, craft, and utilitarian objects. There is also a great variety of materials. As a sample collection we have the Tachibina in their box (paper and textile), the Meiji Tachibina (painted clay), a purse clasp or *kanagu* (metal), a wood-block print or *ukiyo-e* (paper), a hanging scroll or *kakemono* (painting on silk), *netsuke* (*tsuishu* or carved red lacquer), as decoration on an Imari bowl (porcelain), and on a saké cup (red and gold lacquer on a wooden base). These are only a few examples; Tachibina are also found on textiles, inside shells of the shell game, on combs, *inro* and on many other lacquer objects—indeed this frivolous seeming motif is even (but rarely) to be seen on sets of sword furnishings.

The classic Japanese house has a certain small alcove called *tokonoma* for hanging a scroll or *kakemono*. Underneath is displayed an art object; a simple, yet refined flower arrangement completes the decor. According to status and inclination, the family will have a few scrolls or a large collection to choose from. The subject depicted should reflect the seasons, months, some seasonal theme or symbol. Thus a lonely deer and a few coloured maple leaves suggest the melancholy mood of autumn; a fragile butterfly and an open fan would conjure up the heat of summer and a refreshing breeze—there is an added delight for scholars—the Chinese word for fan also means 'to call the wind' and 'to strike a butterfly'. A sober black-and-white poem describes a mountainous winter landscape, as beautiful as its calligraphy. As for spring— what is more representative of spring and the third month than dolls? A flowering prunus branch and a Tachibina pair tell us, like the Biblical Song of Songs that 'flowers have appeared on earth' and that 'the time of singing has returned'.

Dogū and Haniwa figures / Dogū (left): H: 24 cm, W: 16 cm / Haniwa (right): H: 21 cm, W: 11 cm / Baked clay / Private collection.

The oldest representations of the human figure in Japanese history. The heart-shaped owl face and goggle eyes typify the Dogū image, the cylindrical shape and perforated eyes and mouth are characteristic of the more sophisticated Haniwa figure. These two clay figures have the general shape and attitude of Tachibina or standing dolls and justify the talismanic, ancestral and fertility-giving roles ascribed to Tachibina.

Ascetic Buddha / H: 18 cm, W: 11 cm / Rosewood (*shitan*) / Private collection.

One of the rarest representations of the Buddha. — 'He fasted, to the point of death, hoping to free his body, but this trial, too, failed him. . .' In the expression of this Buddha, art and religion have been sublimated to the point of pure spirit.

Kannon / H: 40 cm, W: 30 cm / Cypress wood (*hinoki*); lacquer; metal and glass ornaments; inlaid glass eyes / 18th century / Private collection.

An unusual depiction of Kannon as giver of children.

Jizo / H: 34 cm, W: 24 cm / Stone / INSCR: Meiji 3rd year 6th month 9th day (9th June 1870) / Niigata Prefecture / Private collection.

Jizo as protector and patron saint of children. Three small Kokeshi dolls and food in doll-printed papers have been left with Jizo as consolation for departed children. The stones symbolize prayers and aid for the dead.

Daruma / H: 10 cm, W: 8 cm / Papier-mâché tumbler doll / Private collection.

Avalokitesvara-Sadaksari or Daruma / Print of a Tibetan bronze H: 15 cm, W: 11 cm / Daruma: H: 3 cm, W: 4 cm / Solid lacquer / Ishikawa Prefecture.

A souvenir doll from Ishikawa, which has a well-known lacquer industry. The doll is made of hardened waste material of different colours.

Daruma (double exposure photograph) / H: 10 cm, W: 9 cm / Pine wood (*matsu*) / Private collection.

The roughly carved shape, around which the papier-mâché is pressed to form the toy, has acquired the pleasing patina of age, and is aesthetically more appealing than the colourful end product. The true meaning of *mingei*, of 'objects born, not made', of function and simplicity, is admirably illustrated.

Gosho doll/ H: 10 cm, W: 11 cm / Clay base, *gofun* and colours / Private collection.

The clay Gosho doll is the oldest of its kind. This doll was made in a mould and one hand and foot were made separately. The features are modelled and painted very delicately. It has a more mature expression than most other Gosho dolls.

Gosho dolls / H: 8.5 cm, 5 cm / *Gofun* over pulverized Paulownia wood / Private collection.

Ebisu and Daikoku, two of the Seven Lucky Gods of Japan. Ebisu, carrying a sea bream, represents the riches of the sea; Daikoku, with mallet and sack, represents the wealth of the land.

Gosho dolls for Girls' Day / H: 5 cm, W: 3 cm / Private collection.

Five musicians of a Hina Matsuri set (*gonin bayashi*). The red apron shows the auspicious plum blossom design, emblem of Girls' Day.

Nara doll / H: 20 cm, W: 12 cm / Painted cypress wood (*hinoki*) / Technique: *ittōbori* or one-knife carving / Signed: Hōtō saku (Hōtō carved) / Private collection.

The doll represents a Noh actor playing a Shōjō or drinker, recognizable by his long, red hair and crimson *kimono*. The play tells of a saké seller, who is rewarded by a thirsty Shōjō for giving him all he can drink. The Shōjō bewitches a huge saké jar, so that it will always be full.

When Ieyasu became Shogun in 1603, he decreed Noh the official art of his government.

Noh actor (Okina) / H: 7 cm, W: 5 cm / Carved wood, *gofun*, colours and gold / Private collection.

Saga style doll. The dance of Okina is performed only on special Noh festivals, as the opening act. Originally a religious rite, praying for good fortune and happiness.

Noh actor / H: 24 cm, W: 16 cm / Collection J. Steylaerts, Belgium.

Ishobina or costume doll representing Okina, 'the Good Old Man'. In Noh theatre, the Okina role is the only one in which the mask is put on when the actor is on the stage, facing the audience.

Noh actor / H: 20 cm, W: 18 cm / Collection J. Steylaerts, Belgium.

Ishobina or costume doll representing Waka Onna. The beautiful, stiff and colourful costumes are an integral part of the stylized Noh drama. The red and gold brocade robe is in the *bekko* or tortoiseshell pattern.

Kamo dolls / H: 6 cm, W: 5 cm / 19th century / Willow wood, various textiles / Oyama collection, Tokyo.

A miniature pair of extremely refined and masterfully executed dolls with real hair and finely painted features. The soft, flowing lines of the costumes, made of silk, brocade and crêpe over wood, give the illusion of stuffed bodies, and totally hide the hard material underneath.

Kamo doll / H: 8 cm, W: 4 cm / 19th century / Ivory head and hands, body in kimekomi technique / Oyama collection, Tokyo.

This unique doll is one of the rarest and most unusual of its kind. Remarkable are the finely carved ivory head and hands. Hair, features and feet are lacquered. The costume and pose seem to indicate a Chinese dancer or acrobat. The luxury of the materials—ivory, brocade, gilt base, and the elaborate execution are strong indications that this piece was made to order, perhaps by a sculptor of Buddhist images (*busshi*) or a *netsuke* carver (*netsuke-shi*).

Kimekomi doll / H: 9 cm, W: 5 cm / Private collection.

Very well-made and finished example. The silk used has been dyed and painted to scale. The doll represents a sower scattering seeds, and on his clothes are depicted birds and *naruko* or bird frighteners. Head and hands are *gofun* covered.

Saga doll (Kubifuri Saga—head shaking Saga) / H: 30 cm, W: 16 cm / 18th century / Lacquered wood / Oyama collection, Tokyo.

The figure represents a court or a temple attendant (*doji*) dressed in a richly patterned robe, decorated with gingko leaves. He is a humorous little man, for he shakes his head and puts out his tongue when gently moved. He holds a rooster, symbolic of the third lunar month, when cockfights (Tori Awase) were held at court and in temple grounds. This doll could well have been a present for a boy born in the Year of the Rooster, as the Rooster stands for courage and combativeness.

Kokeshi dolls / Large Akiho, Miyagi Pref. / Small Nambu, Iwate Pref. / L. H: 40 cm, W: 7.5 cm / S. H: 4 cm, W: 1.5 cm / Various woods / Early 20th century / Private collection.

Simple variations on the sphere and cylinder theme, born in the cold and wintry Tohoku region. Playthings, hot-spring souvenirs or memorials to dead children?

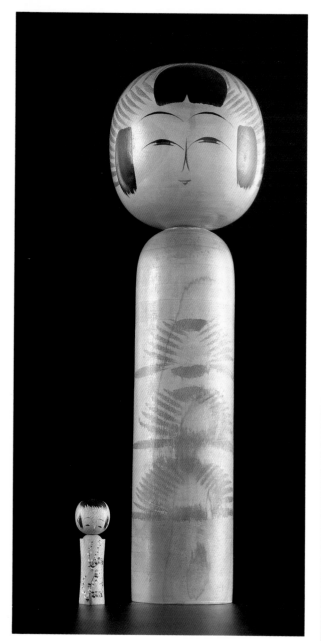

Takeda doll / H: 35 cm, W: 25 cm / Early 19th century Collection Luc and Jessie Sanders, Belgium.

A fine and typical example of the Takeda doll, showing all the characteristics: the extravagant pose, the dynamism, the upturned eyes and the downturned mouth. The orange and green dyed textiles, even the stand with the painted reserve is original. The figure represents a *namban* or foreigner. The face and hands are beautifully modelled. The ruffled collar and pantaloon were attributes of the Dutch and Portuguese but were also worn by Chinese acrobats, dancers and entertainers generally. The models were the puppets and actors of the Takeda theatre in Osaka.

Kyohobina Girls' Day dolls / Emperor: H: 31 cm, W: 28 cm / Empress: H: 30 cm, W: 30 cm / Collection Luc and Jessie Sanders, Belgium.

Emperor and Empress seated on *tatami* dais. Refined features and the matching brocade and orange crêpe costumes are typical for the Kyoto dolls of the 1800's. Note the many layers of the Empress doll's costume (*juni-hitoe*), her Chinese style crown, and the Emperor's feet, *shaku* (baton of office) and curved sword. Although the male figure's head is bigger than the female's, the overall height is exactly the same.

Dairibina (Imperial couple) / Emperor: H: 32 cm, W: 27 cm / Empress: H: 31 cm, W: 25 cm / Kyoto type / Private collection.

The clothes of Hina dolls were inspired by the clothes worn at the Imperial court of Heian times. Typical for the Kyoto style are the five layered, thickly padded dress (*itsutsuginu*) and plain trouser-skirt (*hakama*) of the female doll. The square shape, complicated embroidered central panel (*hirao*) and joined feet typify the male doll.

In Kyoto the Empress was placed to the right of the Emperor.

Dairibina (Imperial couple) / Emperor:H: 35 cm, W: 42 cm / Empress: H: 37 cm, W: 40 cm / Edo type / Private collection.

The narrow eyes, well-defined nose and small mouth, set in an oval face, give these dolls a gentle, refined, and aristocratic expression. The Empress' hands are hidden, the five layered dress suggested by stitched bands. The unpadded edges of the sleeves are beautifully embroidered with flying phoenixes. The crown (*hokan*) is of Chinese inspiration and many statues of Buddhist deities were also embellished with such headdresses. The Emperor wears a lacquered hat (*kanmuri*) with a stiff gauze panel at the back.

In Edo the Empress was placed to the left of the Emperor.

Dairibina (Imperial couple) / Emperor: H: 22 cm, W: 33 cm / Empress: H: 22 cm, W: 20 cm / Meiji type / Private collection.

The male doll has a sumptuous brocade coat (*sokutai*), the sleeves stitched with silk thread. His belt has been simplified, and he is holding the sceptre of office (*shaku*) and wearing his sword (*katana*). The female doll is clothed in an outer *kimono* (*karaginu*), heavily decorated with gold embroidery, tassels, and braid. She has an elaborately painted and threaded court fan (*hiogi*). Although richly made, these dolls lack the noble and spiritual expressions of earlier times.

Kyohobina / H: 30 cm, W: 20 cm / Early 19th century / Collection Luc and Jessie Sanders, Belgium.

This beautifully rendered doll has poise, grace and elegance and a perfect egg-shaped head, once embellished with human hair. Her costume is made of orange embroidered crêpe, blue brocade, and painted gauze. Her features are finely and sensitively painted—she is a true aristocrat among dolls—possibly a standing Empress.

Three Girls' Day dolls / H: 22 cm, W: 15 cm / Collection Luc and Jessie Sanders, Belgium.

Saké pourers (*kanjo*)

Norimono (Palanquin) / Carrying pole: H: 5 cm, L: 92 cm / Palanquin: H: 25 cm, W: 25 cm, L: 32 cm / Black and gold lacquer on wooden base, chased metal fittings / Early 19th century / White Art Centre, Ghent, Belgium.

This miniature *norimono* is part of an unusually large and elaborate Girls' Day set. It is perfect in every detail: the interior is embellished with Tosa paintings, a *tatami* or rice-straw mat, *sudare* or bamboostrip blinds. The lacquered exterior shows the Tokugawa *mon* or heraldic device. *Norimono* were made for special occasions such as marriages in noble families and were forbidden to merchants (1681) and the *samurai* class (1737). Priests and doctors were allowed the use of carrying chairs. The three seated dolls represent the Emperor's lackeys (*shicho*).

A similar piece is illustrated in 'Lacquer, an International History and Collector's Guide, page 101, The Crowood Press'

Girls' Day dolls / H: 26.5 cm / Collection P. de Klark, Belgium.

Heads of the four musicians (enlarged close-up): two hand drum players, one big drum player (with sticks) and one flutist (respectively *ko-tsuzumi*, *ō-tsuzumi*, *taiko*, and *fue*).

These faces are an exercise in physiognomy—the character and temperament of each man can be read and is totally different, yet when they make music together, they are in total harmony. The Edo period dollmaker's message can still be read!

Girls' Day doll / H: 20.5 cm / Collection P. de Klark, Belgium.

The chanter, member of the five musicians (*gonin bayashi*) of the Hina Matsuri set.

Ishobina (costume doll) / H: 15 cm, W: 17 cm / Private collection.

Rakugo or story teller. The *Rakugo* tells comical stories, filled with puns. His fan is a very important accessory, used to imitate all kinds of objects—chopsticks, a pipe, a book or a stick.

Boys' Day doll / H: 42 cm, W: 26 cm / Collection Luc and Jessie Sanders, Belgium.

Yoshitsune. A handsome and idealized hero, and one of Japan's greatest military men, who fell victim to his half-brother's jealousy. He is shown in full battle armour, contemplating death or victory with the impassive face of the true *samurai*.

Boys' Day doll / H: a. 30 cm / Private Collection.

Takenouchi-no-Sukune, a statesman exemplifying the virtues of wisdom, loyalty and integrity. The long, narrow hands and expressive face indicate that this doll was made in the late Edo period.

Ichimatsu doll / H: 35 cm, W: 10 cm / Collection Luc and Jessie Sanders, Belgium.

This doll is wearing the *furisode* or long-sleeved *kimono*, worn by children and unmarried young girls. The textiles are woven, printed and tie-dyed to scale. She has real hair and glass inlaid eyes. The limbs are attached to the body by supple textile joints.

Miniature _inro_ + _netsuke_ / H: 3.5 cm, W: 2.5 cm / Kakihan / H: 3 cm, W: 2 cm / S: Kajikawa / Late 19th century / Kyoto Gallery, Brussels.

These _inro_ and their _netsuke_ were used as miniature accessories for the male Ichimatsu dolls. They are decorated with flowers, leaves, and butterflies in different tones of gold lacquer in relief (_taka maki-e_). The ivory _netsuke_ (right) represents a child playing with a fox mask, like the one on the left.

Tachibina / Female: H: 5.5 cm, W: 1.5 cm / Male: H: 6.5 cm, W: 5 cm / Private collection.

Flat, clay dolls painted red and gold, decorated with wisteria flowers. Illegible stamp of the maker. They are in their original wooden box with a glass top. On the back of the box is written Meiji 45 (Taisho 1) March 3rd Chikanobu Haruko. The coloured label reads Matsuya *gofukuten* (*kimono shop*).

Tachibina / Female: H: 11 cm, W: 3 cm / Male: H: 15 cm, W: 7 cm / Private collection.

Their clothes are made of paper and thin textiles over paper, with painted wisteria flowers. The features are very delicate and the blackened teeth of the female doll are visible; she also has real hair. They are in their original box.

Kakemono (hanging scroll) / H: 117 cm, W: 40 cm / Private collection.

Painting on silk, an elegant and refined rendering of the birth of a year—spring. The magic circle of the seasons, the givers of light and life—sun and moon, and, centrally the figures of man and woman, so that the cycle may blossom . . . and bear fruit . . .

Tachibina / H: 5 cm, W: 4 cm / *Netsuke*—boxwood (*tsuge*), inlaid ivory faces / S: Kazuo (Mizutani) / Collection J.W.

PART II
The MOTIF

OKIMONO

The so-called golden age of the *netsuke* came to a gradual stop in 1850. With the introduction of Western clothes, the traditional costume for men was abandoned, and with it the *inro* and *netsuke*, two magnificent forms of miniature art. The art of the *netsuke* did not stop abruptly, once and for all—it languished. Allowing a few rare exceptions, *netsuke* were no longer made for enjoyable and practical daily use, or for aesthetic and artistic appreciation, as before. They dropped to the level of commercially made, stale repetitions of existing pieces.

The West had discovered the ivory sculpture of the East. The question is, how many amateurs recognized, appreciated and estimated at their just value the genius and inspiration, the untiring effort and technical skill, developed by generations of carvers? The West was a new and undiscerning market demanding anything and everything oriental. All porcelain was called "Chinaware", *netsuke* were sold as "Mandarin or Japanese buttons" and the art of lacquering became "Japanning". "Chinoiserie" was "à la mode"! The West wanted impressive and complicated pieces—hence the birth of the ivory export *okimono*. It is best defined as an exclusively decorative object, its sole purpose being to please the eye. (*oki*=place, *mono*=object)

The Japanese generally prefer simple wood, bronze, or porcelain pieces for display in the *tokonoma*, although ivory pieces exist of a sublime simplicity, illustrating superbly the art of understatement, of eliminating every superfluous detail until only the essential purity of form and line is left over. It must be remarked here that the Japanese artist was unequalled in the arts of miniaturization and symbolization, and that one or both of these two supporting factors of his work fell away in the case of the *okimono*. The export *okimono* was considered more as a proof of virtuosity than as an artistic achievement. No difficulty was too great—no problem was beyond a solution: one could even say that difficulties were expressly sought so that the artist could prove his total mastery of tools and material. He carved fishermen with realistic, extremely fine nets, complete with fish and struggling octopuses, peddlers carrying a dozen differently woven baskets, *geisha* with elaborate hairdos, baskets of flowers and intricately engraved clothes, birds with each feather made separately, crabs with articulated pincers.

These *okimono* were undoubtedly well-made, even with a certain flamboyance meant to astound and overwhelm the onlooker, but often at the cost of sensibility. The symbolism apparent to a Japanese only, the delicate or hidden sense of humour so often found in *netsuke* and ivory works for the domestic market, were sadly lacking in the export pieces, leading to the general opinion that all Japanese ivory sculpture was artificial and contrived. What is deemed artistic by one generation is often ridiculed by the next, but rediscovered many decades later when norms and perspectives have changed. The Japanese carver put into his *okimono* what he thought the foreigner expected to find: painstaking attention to detail and exaggerated technical prowess resulting in a frankly decorative piece. This is perhaps the right moment to ask ourselves how many contemporary artists are capable of original ideas and the same degree of craftsmanship.

The examples shown represent personages not readily recognizable by the uninitiated, and if bought by a Westerner, it would be on their decorative merit only; but a Japanese would at once see their symbolism and grant them the privilege of being displayed in the *tokonoma* on Boys' Day. The swordsmith identified by his triangular hat made of lacquered paper, a sign of his art, has made a miniature suit of armour (*yoroi*) for his grandson. Its least detail is accurate, from the combat helmet (*kabuto*) to the battle insignia of a commander (*saihai*), waved proudly by the boy. His sister, sitting on the ground, offers the all-important *samurai* sword. When he was five years old the Japanese boy wore a *mamori katana*, a miniature sword wrapped in brocade as a protective amulet against illness and accidents; if he was the son of a *samurai* he received the suit of armour and two small swords bearing the heraldic signs of his family (*mon*); at the age of fifteen (*gempuku*) the swords were exchanged for the ones he would carry during his lifetime and in his turn pass on to his son.

The swordsmith was one of the most respected artisans in Japan and even the highborn did not find it beneath their dignity to learn the secrets of sword-making. The tempering of a sword by a master, assisted by his apprentices, was a quasi-religious rite, undertaken only on auspicious days, after fasting and prayers to the gods (*kami*) who protected the emplacement of the forge. The distinctive triangular hat worn by Shinto priests and exorcists for purification rites was also worn by all assistants. A plaited straw rope (*shimenawa*) marking a sacred spot, was placed across the entry to keep evil spirits at bay. The most famous school of armourers was undoubtedly the Myochin; for many generations the members of this family made some of the finest swords, masks, armours and sword furniture ever seen. Their hereditary line continued unbroken for seven hundred years and they were armourers to the Imperial court from the twelfth to the eighteenth century.

Despite its many details the carving still gives the impression of lightness due to its elongation and the vertical elegance of the upswept curves in the clothing. The faces are expressive, the figures animated, the little soldier serious and already aware of his importance, the old man proud of his grandson and drawing all attention to the small boy by his upward directed gaze and gesture, the smiling little girl with her round chubby cheeks and the high painted eyebrows of the aristocrat, timidly holding up the sword. They are all happy and untroubled by the grim spectre of war represented by the iron battle mask (*somen*)

behind them, a masterpiece of metal art.

The second *okimono* misses the vitality and impression of lightness of the first. It is a broad and powerful group, massively constructed and carved. The artist was obviously at his best in the execution of profuse detail. While the clothes are strongly and deeply incised and draped, the faces have little personality and the hands are insensitive and weakly executed. All the static energy of the piece comes from the skillful and baroque play of the rich and varied rhythm of the clothing.

The expression "by Jingo" is often used by the English to express surprise. And a surprising woman she was. When her husband, the Emperor Chuai, died after refusing to obey the gods' order to conquer Korea, she set out herself, even though she was pregnant. She was accompanied by her minister Takenouchi no Sukune, a wise and capable statesman and warrior, said to have been advisor to six successive rulers. Fortune favoured the expedition and legend tells that all the gods came to her aid, Ryujin, the Dragon King of the Sea, lending her his tide-ruling jewels. The Korean king submitted without a battle and she returned to Japan with an enormous treasure consisting of gold, silver, precious textiles and many hostages. She then gave birth to her son Homuda, the future emperor Ojin, whose birth she had delayed by wearing a large stone tied inside her belt.

While the Empress Jingu was regent, Takenouchi no Sukune became the tutor of the young prince. Jingu Kogo is the only woman admitted to the Boys' Day display, because of her courage and military exploits. Although the etymology of the word is different, her name also lives on in the word "*jingoism*", it was coined by the British and is defined as extreme nationalism marked by a belligerent foreign policy. It could well be applied to this military Empress. She is always shown in full battle armour, wearing a headband and holding a military fan (*gunbai*) and armed with the long sword (*jindachi*) in a fur scabbard. She is often depicted with her minister, who personifies loyalty and integrity. He is holding her son, the baby emperor.

Ojin is often identified with Hachiman, the god of war. This is surprising, as no bellicose activities, either aggressive or defensive, are ascribed to him. On the contrary it was during his reign that writing, sericulture, weaving, dyeing, and Confucian learning were brought to Japan by Wani in 285. He was a famous Korean scholar from the state of Paekche and his innovations had a marked civilizing impact on Japanese life. The Empress Jingu (Regent 201–269), her son, the Emperor Ojin (270–310), and Hachiman, the god of war (here he seems to be a distinctly different personality), are revered at the Usa Shrine, Oita Prefecture. They were so highly esteemed that Imperial delegates were regularly sent to the shrine to report on the state of the country's affairs.

The 'Wei Chih' (Chinese chronicles) mention that the men of Wo or Wa (Japan) paid regular tribute to Lo-lang (a Han colony in Korea), and that there was communication between the Wei dynasty and Yamatai or

Yamato (the ancient name of Japan). The 'Nihongi' mentions the sending of troops to Korea in 369, and a Korean memorial refers to the fighting between the state of Koguryo and the men of Wa. In 391 Yamatai annexed the kingdoms of Paekche, Kaya, and Silla. At this time ideographic script came to Japan in the form of Confucian works. Artisans, weavers, smiths and agricultural experts migrated to Japan. The legends related to the Empress Jingu and her son Ojin could have their base in these historic facts.

THE WHITE HORSE

As the Empress Jingu is the only woman honoured in the Boys' Day display, so the white horse is the only animal permitted as the symbol of valour and endurance. *Tango no sekku* is the usual name for the Boys' Festival. 'Tango' literally means 'first horse day'. It is indeed a wonderful horse. Its rider is invisible—like Pegasus it is the steed of the gods. A horse was a valuable possession, used mostly by messengers and in war time. Horse sacrifice was forbidden in the late Yayoi period. The rich were transported in carrying chairs (*kago*) and the court nobles in palanquins (*norimono*) or oxdrawn carts (*ushi-* or *goshoguruma*). White horses, the ultimate in beauty, value and preciosity were given to Shinto shrines as votive offerings, and shrines, to this day, have a stable for the horse of the gods. Only the rich could afford such a gift, other people gave paintings of white horses (*ema*), literally 'horse-pictures', to entreat and thank the gods.

Sei Shonagon in '*The Pillow Book*' mentions the festival of the Blue Horses on the seventh day of the first month. This ceremony in which twenty-one horses from the Imperial stables were paraded before the Emperor was an ancient Chinese custom, brought to Japan in the early eighth century. It was the usage to give outstanding horses to the Emperor as a token of friendship or as a sign of submission by vassals. The original horses had been steel-grey, but such horses were always exceedingly rare. White was the colour of purity according to Shinto ritual, and in the tenth century the 'blue' horses were replaced by white ones.

Note: That the Chinese loved horses is evident in their sensitive paintings and the realistically and admirably rendered tomb horses of the T'ang dynasty (618–907). The sense of vitality, of harnessed power is a necessary element in the appreciation of Chinese art. The Musée Guimet, Paris, possesses a superb and rare painting "The Kirghizes presenting horses to Chienlung" executed in Chinese style by the Jesuit priest-artist Castiglione. Horses were precious tributes and the Manchu Emperor obviously wanted to record his moment of triumph for posterity. Nothing comparable to the Chinese rendering of painted or ceramic horses exists anywhere else in the world.

MODELS FOR OKIMONO

When *okimono* for export were much in demand, as was the case in the Meiji and Taisho periods, it was customary for merchants to commission ivory carvers to work for them, and also to furnish them with the crude ivory. Wooden models, drawings, and printed books all furnished popular subject matter for carvers with good technical skills, lacking inspiration and originality of vision. Hokusai's "*Manga*" was much consulted and the "*Bambutsu Zukai Isai Gashiki*" (Isai's Designs for Everything) was also a rich source for craftsmen, with designs ranging from lacquer combs (*kushi*) to iron swordguards (*tsuba*)!

For an order of a determined number of identical pieces, a standard procedure consisted of furnishing one bronze or wooden figure made by a well-known sculptor, or a master would carve an example in wood, indicating engraved patterns in different colours. His apprentices would then carve the figure as close to the original as possible, with allowance for a minimum of individual expression. Where needed, the master would then correct or add some finishing touches. He also permitted his pupils to sign the best pieces with his name, which was considered an honour.

This explains why there are quite a number of identical *okimono* and *netsuke* on the world market. Either they were produced by the described method or copied from older pieces. A copy was not looked upon disparagingly—on the contrary it was a necessary lesson for learning difficult techniques, and was considered an achievement when well-executed.

OF NETSUKE AND DOLLS

Dollmakers made *netsuke* and *netsuke* carvers made dolls. It is more likely that *netsuke* carvers were inspired by the variety of dolls and puppets, and the many possibilities of decorative treatment they offered, than that many dollmakers resorted to carving miniatures of their products in wood or ivory. Toys are necessarily smooth and soft, so children will not be hurt when playing, smooth, rounded surfaces are the most agreeable tactile qualities of a *netsuke*. Among *netsuke* carvers and collectors, doll and toy *netsuke* form an amusing and original category with which could be formed an extensive and didactic miniature collection.

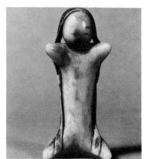

"*The Netsuke Handbook*" of Ueda Reikichi offers interesting information concerning dolls and *netsuke*. He tells us that one of the earliest artists in this domain was the *netsuke* carver Nonoguchi Ryuho (1594–1669). 'He was nicknamed "Hinaya" (dollmaker) because his vocation was the creation of fine dolls. Extant examples of his work are very scarce'. 'Chikayuki Fukushima (1837–1883) who lived at Asakusa in Tokyo, excelled at making Asakusa dolls (carved Noh actors) but was also a carver of *netsuke*'.

One anecdote about an artist from Osaka named Shugetsu (active in the Meiwa period) is worth recalling. He must have been an all-round artist as he was famous as a painter in the style of the Kano school, earning the title of '*hogen*' (second honorary art title given by the Emperor, a Buddhist title meaning Eye of the Law) and as a *netsuke* carver of extraordinary ability and refinement. He went to Edo to make his fortune and opened a doll shop in Jikkenmise. He created original Hina doll sets and added decorative cherry and mandarin orange trees, suggesting the decor of the Shishinden Hall of the Imperial Palace. It was an offence to portray sacred objects and he was imprisoned. Later he was exiled from Edo. He returned to Osaka and *netsuke* carving.... Perhaps he then carved doll *netsuke* ... or made dolls with ivory heads....

His adopted son, Shugetsu II, also made Hina dolls and helmeted dolls (*kabuto ningyō*), the suits of armour and the war helmet itself for Boys' Day, as well as festival carriages for dolls. Of Shugetsu IV it is said that besides Hina dolls and *netsuke*, he carved *okimono* in ivory and Chinese woods for export (Meiji period).

Another Japanese source (T. Kitamura) mentions Yamada Tokubei as 'making exquisite Hina doll sets with heads, hands and accessories in sculptured ivory'. These are only a few examples of artists who made the whole doll themselves, who practised the arts of doll making and *netsuke* carving with equal mastery. They furnish the proof that there ARE elaborate dolls with ivory heads and hands (Suntory Museum, Tokyo)—that there ARE entire Hina sets carved in ivory (The Makino

Collection, Tokyo, possesses an ivory Hina set consisting of 15 figures and the accessories by Kikuchi Godo). But these cases are more the exception than the rule.

It is noteworthy that from their origins until the Genroku period, Girls' Day dolls, and even more particularly, Boys' Day dolls became increasingly taller and ever more luxurious and imposing—and accordingly more expensive. The Shogun Yoshimune put a stop to this frivolous expenditure by his edicts, which, among others, limited the size of dolls to 20 cm. Wise dollmakers took revenge by making extraordinarily small, exquisite, and costly examples!

Unless the master dollmaker made the entire doll personally on some dignitary's or rich merchant's order, and signed the finished piece or its box, it is probable that the doll is the end product of a chain of people working together, each one specializing in a specific phase of the work. Some made and painted the heads and hands, others modelled bodies, implanted hair, glued and embroidered the clothes, and still others made the tiny accessories such as fans, swords, crowns and musical instruments. The fine quality miniature lacquered furniture was made by lacquer artists. It was (and still is) customary to work in such a way in Japan. In analogy with the European painter's atelier, a master in any art always had pupils learning their trade, working for him over a long period of time. But the work of a team will always be secondary compared to the work of the single artist who is capable of conceiving and executing his personal vision with skill and sensibility.

Note: *Netsuke* and *inro* have been so much publicized by excellent books, record prices at auction sales, and world conventions, that it is difficult to imagine that any connoisseur of Japanese art ignores their existence or function. They are an art in themselves, a unique form of Japanese creativity, and when one counts the working hours (at today's cost) of the time spent carving a delightful and expressive miniature, an original *ojime* (slide bead) and the elaboration of a lacquer *inro*—painted, carved and inlaid— plus the rare materials sometimes used, we must admit that seemingly exorbitant is still cheap.

The etymology of the word *netsuke* is *ne*=root, *tsuke*=attachment. As the roots keep a tree attached to the ground, so the *netsuke* acts as counterweight to the *inro*, a seal or medicine box, and various other objects—purses (*kinchaku*), pipe-cases (*kiseruzutsu*), and tobacco pouches (*tabako-ire*), known as *sagemono* or hanging things. The Japanese *kimono* has no pockets, so, in earlier times all utilitarian objects were suspended from the textile belt or *obi*. In the late 16th and early 17th centuries the *netsuke* grew from a strangely formed natural object into a beautifully decorated toggle worn by the *samurai* and merchant class to underline their wealth and status.

The types of *netsuke* can be generally classified into *katabori* or figure carving representing natural objects such as the human figure, animals and flowers, or manmade objects. *Manju* or round rice cake shape, ranging from simple in one piece, to two elaborately decorated fitting halves. Variants of this type are the *ryusa*, a hollowed-out and intricately carved round, oval or rectangular *netsuke* and the *kagamibuta*, in wood or ivory with a metal plate insert, made by metal artists or swordsmiths. The *sashi netsuke* is an unusually long *netsuke* thrust into the *obi*, a variant being the *obihasami* with a hook on one end, which fits over the lower edge of the *obi*. The most currently used materials are wood, ivory and stag antler; the rarest include hornbill, rhinoceros horn, amber, narwhal and walrus tooth.   Raymond Bushell is also a collector of dolls in his specialized sphere: *netsuke*.   Those represented here have been chosen for three reasons—variety of subject, material and rarety.

In the context of *netsuke* and dolls, I would like to render homage to two great contemporary Japanese artists.   Both have individuality, universal appeal and artistic integrity.   Jusaburo Tsujimura is a creator and his dolls are art.   Kodo Okuda is an eminent lacquerer and also a carver of *netsuke*; his art is pure poetry.   Both men dare to be different . . . .

UJI

Uji, near Nara, is famous for its tea.   From the wood of the teabush (*cha-no-ki*) is produced a somewhat rustic cousin to the Nara doll, the woman teapicker doll.   It is carved in the *ittō-bori* manner, is simple and unpretentious and painted in soft hues.   Ueda Reikichi ascribes this doll to Kanamori Shigechika (1583–1656) (His '*go*' or art name was Sowa).   He was the Daimyo of Ida but relinquished his office to become a priest.   When retired he lived in a suburb of Uji and was well-known as a tea ceremony master.   As a hobby he carved miniature figures of the local women out of teabush wood (a fitting pastime for a teamaster!).   His technique was elegant and his carvings were known as Uji *ningyō*.

His seventh or eighth generation descendant Kamibayashi Keimei (1801–1870) (*go:* Gyuka) revived and refined this carving technique when, in 1843 he was asked to carve a typical Uji souvenir for presentation to the Shogun by Tsumura, the Lord of Ise, who was also magistrate of Kyoto.   An Uji doll was presented to the Shogun and several *daimyo* found the carving so interesting that they asked Gyuka to carve the same subject for them.   He had served the family of one of the imperial princes as a priest in 1819 and was a fervent supporter of the Emperor. He used all his influence and power to keep the best tea grown in the Uji district for the exclusive use of the Imperial family and away from the Tokugawa shogunate.

The teabush (Camellia sinensis) is a small, evergreen shrub, and gives only limited scope for sculpture.   Obviously the dolls are restricted in size and detail to a strict minimum.

IMARI

The earliest Japanese pottery dates from the Neolithic or Jomon ('coiled rope') period, named after the particular vessels, inspired by basket-work. The middle Jomon period produced the strange Dogū figurines and during the Yayoi period unadorned pottery and Haniwa figures were made. Then, well-known to every connoisseur, are the Six Ancient Kilns: Bizen, Echizen, Seto, Shigaraki, Tamba and Tokoname. Their simple pottery products were made mostly for household and farm use, particularly as storage jars for rice, tea-leaves, and other daily necessities. These kilns were most conservative as to their techniques, shapes and materials and from the Momoyama period to this day, any old object suitable for the tea ceremony is much prized.

Porcelain proper has a history dating back to the beginning of the seventeenth century when, after Toyotomi Hideyoshi's ill-fated Korean venture, many potters were brought back to Japan. They had a superior knowledge of pottery-making inherited from the Chinese and ceramic art flourished in Japan due to their efforts. It was a Korean named Ri Sanpei who discovered *kaolin*, the clay needed to make fine porcelain, in the Arita district of Kyushu. Tengudani was the first kiln to produce porcelain (1616).

This porcelain is called Imari ware after the port from which it was exported to Europe by the Dutch. It has been said that most Imari was made for export (and thus in bad taste). The fact is that the greatest part was made for domestic use. This is evident in the refined blue-and-white wares and the specific shapes of covered rice and soup bowls, *soba* cups, pickle and soya-sauce dishes, saké cups and stands, all of which were certainly not used in Europe. The majority of Edo merchants liked colourful and gilded pieces just as much as the Europeans liked 'exotic' wares; there are good and bad pieces on both sides of the ocean.

Late seventeenth and eighteenth century production tended to be constant in quality of paste and decoration but in the nineteenth century there was a general decline due to excessive demand; the paste became greyish and the decor overworked. During the Meiji period, Arita produced mediocre Nagasaki ware for export. Some examples, however, show the boldness of design and colour, the freedom and fantasy of the decorator, which are charming without rivalling in the least with the more sophisticated and powerful Chinese and Korean products. There are two notable exceptions to this rule: Kakiemon and Nabeshima ware, the best examples of which may be counted among the finest porcelain in the world.

Kizaimon Sakaida perfected the *aka-e* or red overglaze after many

years of experimenting with a formula bought from a Chinese potter. His first present to the Daimyo was a porcelain *kaki* or persimmon in the new colour; in appreciation his lord bestowed on him the name Kakiemon. The thirteenth generation Kakiemon is still making this delicate and classic ware. Nabeshima was produced in an *oniwa-gama* or garden kiln by Korean potters for the personal use of the Daimyo of Saga, Lord Nabeshima, and for presentation to high-ranking officials. All pieces showing the slightest flaw were broken. Garden kilns were situated within the boundaries of the lord's domain and strictly guarded to prevent transmission of methods to other kilns. This porcelain too is still made by Imaemon, a descendant of the original potters.

Hirado was also a garden kiln and produced a remarkable blue-and-white hand-painted decor of *karako* or playing Chinese children. Tradition has it that the potters who had been separated from their families in Korea developed this design in memory of their kinsfolk, an echo of their sadness and longing for their loved ones. One man, Hirado Gasho, a 'Living Cultural Asset' still produces this pattern by hand.

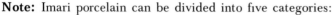

Note: Imari porcelain can be divided into five categories:
Sometsuke: blue and white
Kakiemon: first executed ca 1646—typical orange-red overglaze and other colours—
    delicately decorated on white background
Kinrande: gold on red enamel background; Kutani also uses this glaze
Sansai: three colour overglaze, red and green enamel on white; underglaze blue or
    dullish purple with overglaze red on white
Gosai: five colour or *nishikide* (brocade) from late Ming and early Ch'ing designs.

MASHIKO

Mashiko, in Tochigi Prefecture, had a long tradition of ceramic activity even before the arrival of the famed Hamada Shōji. The potting town was declining rapidly, and the old and time consuming methods were falling into disuse, when the master potter revived many traditional (*dento*) techniques, combining with great sensibility, texture, glaze, and simplicity of line. His work has made him famous in Japan, and indeed, the whole world. No amateur of Japanese pottery ignores his name. With Yanagi Sōetsu and Bernard Leach, he promoted a renewed interest in 'Mingei' or 'people's art', and was a founding member of the first folk art museum in Japan, the Mingeikan in Tokyo. In 1920 he worked with Bernard Leach at St-Ives, England and they established a joint kiln at Mashiko in 1934. Mashiko owes much to the renown of these men and a few (too few, alas) contemporary artists who continue and preserve their legacy.

On the whole, Mashiko is today, one huge commercialized pottery, exploiting former glory. In this century, when all has been sacrificed to materialism, it is paradoxical to see the influential elbow each other aside to buy creations of artists and artisans who had nothing to speak for them except their integrity and honesty in expressing themselves. But one cannot buy integrity by proxy. Bernard Leach in his autobiography '*Beyond East and West*' speaks of his desire to recapture some of the lost values through the use of his own hands, and of his constant search for truth. A passage worth quoting for future student potters, and eminently applicable to all forms of art is the following: 'Periodically I talked to them as they learnt their alphabets of clay—its qualities—its innate demands on a potter—its form and decoration—kilns, slips, glazes,—encouraging them to stand on their own feet, both technically and aesthetically, insisting on right standards but avoiding rules.'

In this and every age there are artists of extraordinary stature, who give the sublime to the world. They are always rare. Next to the giants, there is the supporting cast, the artisans who do their work with respect, knowledge, and love for their material, knowing that all things have their reason for being. To imagine one without the other in the world of art, is as ridiculous as a Seiji Ozawa trying to make music without an orchestra. Without artists to colour our world with beauty, we would see only the black and the white. We need both visionary and realist, stars and bread.

UKIYO-E

The word *ukiyo-e* denotes the 'floating' or 'transitory' world, and what is more ephemeral than the make-believe world of bought pleasures? First linked to the Buddhist principle of the transience of life, the term took on a new meaning in the seventeenth century, and was applied to the assortment of wood-block prints depicting the most popular amusements of the Edo period. Printed books with stories and black and white pictures, Kabuki actors, theatre prints (*shibai-e*), famous courtesans of the Yoshiwara district, prints of *sumo* wrestlers (*sumo-e*), waitresses of fashionable tea-shops and portraits of beautiful women (*bijinga*), made their appearance. Series of landscape prints, of which the greatest exponents were Katsushika Hokusai and Ando Hiroshige, showed the Japanese, who were always enthusiastic travellers on their home ground, splendid views of their country. Their bird-and-flower prints were also masterly, and the great Utamaro's career began with illustrations for poetry books, such as "*The Book of Insects*" (*Ehon mushi erami*) and "*A Chorus of Birds*" (*Momochidori kyoka awase*). Many artists catered to the taste for erotica or '*shunga*' poetically entitled 'Pictures of Spring'.

The wood-block print was a team product: the publisher commissioned, the artist designed, the carver cut the design in numerous blocks of wood, and the printer made the final picture. Around 1660, Hishikawa Moronobu initiated the uncoloured, single print, and in the middle of the eighteenth century, Okumura Masanobu was using up to three blocks to produce '*beni-e*' or red pictures. The colouring technique is ascribed to Suzuki Harunobu, and appeared around 1769. The forty following years were the most prolific and technically perfect in the history of print-making. In its golden days, the print had fifteen different colours, and for each colour another block was needed; embossing, lacquering, and mica sprinkling provided more special effects.

The wood-block picture was not regarded as high art, in spite of the outstanding skills required of all persons involved in the production of a good print. Painting was a refined and aristocratic art—the print was meant for the masses, the commoners. But, then as now, the people had their actor heroes, favourite *sumo* wrestlers, beautiful courtesans, who provided the latest scandals and fashions. It was a popular art, frankly commercial, unpretentious and fresh.

The art declined seriously when Japan was finally opened to foreign trade by Admiral Perry in 1854; Yokohama was designated as the port-of-call and a few Japanese artists continued the production of modern themes in a naive manner: stone houses, Western dress, steamships, trains, and stations in gaudy aniline dyes—Yokohama-*e* or pictures of Yokohama. They have a certain documentary value, but their only charm lies in their amusing and quaint rendering of foreign objects. Be it said for Japanese wood-block prints that they exercised a tangible influence on the European Impressionist school, which admired their boldness of colour and composition. They remain for all time, witnesses of the vitality of the gay and prosperous Edo era.

KABUKI

That Kabuki theatre was immensely popular among the townspeople is attested by the great number of existing wood-block prints (*ukiyo-e*) representing the idols of the day in their best-known roles. Artists devoted much of their time and effort to producing theatrical portraits, as each actor had his fans and followers. Dollmakers followed their example and made doll images of famous actors in heroic pose. Kabuki, with its aura of glamour, gorgeous costumes and dramatic stage effects must have appealed greatly to both masses and prosperous merchant class of the Edo period (1615–1868). It was spectacle, dance and music, brilliant lights and colours, with romantic intrigue more readily understandable than the austere and sober Noh, which always kept its religious undertones. It was as different as a Rodgers and Hart musical compared to a Shakespearean drama. Although a woman, Okuni of Kyoto, masquerading as a man, was at the origin of the Kabuki tradition (1586), actresses were, by a government decree, forbidden to perform because of their extra-curricular activities (1629). Young men were soon banned for the same reason, and only adult men, known as 'onnagata' or female impersonators, were allowed to play women's roles. It is perhaps ironic to note that many women went to see the *onnagata* perform, so that they could learn how to be more feminine.

The famed twelfth century heroes Yoshitsune and Benkei are usually depicted as befits fighting men and military generals, in full battle armour. Benkei is the smallest figure, although he was said to have been eight feet tall and as strong as a hundred men while Yoshitsune was quite small; but legend has a way of enlarging upon the exploits of its children throughout the years and enhancing them with extraordinary powers and prowess. The height could indicate the difference in status between master and retainer. Yoshitsune wears full battle regalia and Benkei is often shown with seven weapons. The seven weapons served the purpose of attacking *samurai* who crossed Gojo Bridge in Kyoto, for Benkei had sworn to take a thousand *samurai* swords. Here Yoshitsune having been mistaken for a woman, kicked Benkei's lance and beat him in the fight that followed. Benkei swore lifelong loyalty to him.

The representation shows Kabuki actors playing the well-known

Kanjincho episode (The Subscription List), and the role of master and servant has been reversed. Benkei is the heroic figure here without any doubt. In 1887, the famous Kabuki actor Danjuro IX was accorded the honour of a command performance before the Emperor—the first time this had ever happened in the history of Kabuki theatre—and his choice was the role of Benkei in Kanjincho, one of the eighteen brilliant Danjuro plays reserved exclusively for his family ('18 Favourite Plays').

The audience participates intensely during a Kabuki performance. At a certain moment when suspense reaches its peak, the actor assumes a pose, called a '*mie*', calculated to impression and enthusiasm the spectators to the highest degree. Strange as it may seem, it was also a part of the *mie* to cross the eyes, and many wood-block artists adopted this manner of facial expression in their work to give more life to their models.

This, then is the moment of the *mie*, reflected in the grim expression of Benkei, who knows that their lives depend upon his acting. When Yoshitsune was fleeing from the unmerited jealousy and anger of his half brother Yoritomo, to seek refuge in the castle of the Daimyo of Oshu, Hidehira, his party disguised as travelling monks (*yamabushi*), was stopped in Kaga (Ataka), by a troop of Yoritomo's soldiers commanded by Sayemon Togashi who refused to let them pass and threatened to behead the whole party if proof of their identity was not produced. Benkei took a roll of paper from his sleeve and pretended to read a letter from the abbot of Hoko-ji asking them to collect funds for the reconstruction of the Todai-ji of Nara. Here versions differ: one says that Sayemon knew who they were but did not want to take them prisoner as he admired their courage—the other says that Yoshitsune burst out laughing at Benkei's performance and was promptly given a few hard slaps as punishment for his irreverent and impolite behaviour. This act would convince any official or *samurai*, as hitting a superior was an offence punishable by immediate death. They were allowed to pass . . . .

KATAGAMI

The *katagami* or literally 'pattern paper' is another virtually unknown example of the patience, skill and sense of balance of the Japanese craftsman. Its invention is ascribed to Yuzen Miyazaki, an artist-painter of the Genroku period (1688–1703) living in Kyoto. He also gave his name to the dyeing-process (Yuzen-dyeing) and to the completed textile product (Yuzen). If it is not proven that he actually invented the *katagami*, he certainly did invent resist dyeing.

The making and preparing of the stencil-paper, the drawing and cutting of the design, the reinforcing of the paper with oil and lacquer, threads or gauze, the dyeing and washing, is a long and arduous, time-consuming process, to say the very least.

The production of a stencil begins with the paper made of mulberryfibre (Broussonetia papyrifera) given strength and hardness by placing the fibres at angles so that they run in three different directions, and a treatment with persimmon juice. It was made waterproof by an application of hard-drying oil and in later times, lacquer.

A design was then placed on top of a few sheets of the paper, firmly secured, and the cutting with extremely strong, sharp knives began. For small, neat holes a punch was used. Very delicate stencils with wide apart motifs were joined by a network of fine silk threads, pasted between two sheets of the paper, when the cutting was finished; later, thin gauze lacquered to one side of the paper only, was used.

The stencil was then ready for use on silk or cotton and, less currently, on linen and leather. The technique on leather, named inden, differs because lacquer is used instead of paint and the stencils are small and very simple, usually geometrical in design.

Two effects could be obtained with one stencil: colour on a white background and white on a coloured background. The first was by applying colour directly, the second by applying resist paste, dyeing the cloth, and then washing the paste away. The colours most favoured were blue and white, but other tints could be added by repeating the process with supplementary stencils in which different parts were cut away. The cloth could be further embellished with painted and embroidered details. A very fine patterned *kimono* fabric, dyed with intricate stencils is known as *komon* (small pattern) characterized by uniform small dots and naturalistic floral design.

KANAGU

An imperial decree of 1873 prohibited the carrying of swords. Suddenly, all those employed in the manufacture of sword furniture saw this source of income drop to zero. The sword had been the all-important part of the *samurai*'s apparel and a sign of his superior caste in which he invested a large amount of money (be it for show or because his life depended on it).

During the peaceful Edo era, the sword was no longer a combat weapon, but a status symbol, and the metalworkers had combined their best technical and artistic skills in producing the miniature metal masterpieces needed to satisfy the important demand. The *samurai* or military class had become gradually impoverished, first without masters, then without wars to fight, at last, even without swords.

A fresh market was sought—and found—in the prosperous merchant class, which wielded financial power. The introduction of tobacco, and of course, the smoking habits of the Portuguese, in 1543, had from then on, created new possibilities for the metalworkers. Every fashionable smoker felt obliged to purchase various pipes, small portable ones complete with cases and tobacco pouches or boxes, and big elaborate ones for smoking at home, some so big that they could do double duty as weapons!

Wood-block prints show the courtesans of the Yoshiwara district smoking long pipes with their customers. Tobacco, despite its exorbitant price, became the craze of the day. Again metalworkers exercised their best efforts in the production of pipes, clasps for various pouches and purses, *ojime* and *netsuke*, including the *kagamibuta* type, in which a beautifully decorated disc is set in a round wood or ivory frame. Well-known artists and even the famed Myochin school deigned to produce these small objects.

The *kanagu* or metalwork on the tobacco pouch or purse, is yet another example of the mastery with which Japanese craftsmen adapted their art to unusual shapes and to objects for everyday use. The metalworking techniques were varied, used singly or in combination with each other. *Niku-bori* was high relief, *taka niku-bori*, a very high relief technique, *katagiri-bori* was a style of carving imitating brush-strokes in *sumi-e* or ink painting.

To give different colours, pure metals such as gold, silver and copper, and metal alloys were used. Currently used as a background was *shakudo*, an alloy of gold and copper given a deep blue-black patina by treatment with chemicals, and *shibuichi*, an alloy of silver and copper, resulting in shades of grey; *shirogane* or white metal was obtained from lead ore and silver; fine details and inlay were usually in pure gold and silver. The *uraza* or metal plate under the flap is sometimes engraved and signed.

The range of subject matter and mastery of material is unbelievable-treatment can be summary, calculated to be effective when seen from a distance, but it can also be so elaborate and delicate that a magnifying glass is needed to appreciate its finest points. The clasps for tobacco pouches show two such extremes. The one showing the puppeteer in formal dress (*kami-shimo*) working a stick puppet on a stand, is so perfectly executed as to be almost too refined, but is saved from mannerism by the enthusiastic and happy expression of the puppeteer; his open mouth and the movement of the puppet-lady, looking back at him over her shoulder, seem to indicate a dialogue between them. The balance and proportion of the subject on the irregularly shaped background is perfect, and the head of the puppet standing high and free, draws the attention first and leads back to the face of the man. From all points of view it is a miniature masterpiece.

The other clasp showing the Tachibina pair is not so skilfully executed as to the metalwork, but it is a very clever grouping of various triangles, resulting in a most agreeable effect. The artist has extended and filled the space of his composition with two clam shells and a cherry blossom and bud at the base. He has also used artistic licence in stretching the form of the female doll, which should normally be much smaller than the male figure. Notwithstanding the soft, rather blurred impression, it is a simple but harmonious and well-composed clasp.

Note: The most famous wood-block artist of all time, Hokusai, designed an unusual and richly coloured *surimono* (a commissioned, limited edition print) entitled '*The Puppeteer and Spear Dancer*' (1820). A puppeteer wearing a luxurious brocade costume is kneeling behind a checkered *goban* or low table on which the game of Go is played. He is manipulating a tall, beautifully dressed female puppet performing the Spear Dance. The Go table, available in most affluent houses, seems to have served as an improvised stage for puppets, when a puppeteer was called upon to perform in private on festive occasions.

SAKÉ

In the legendary stage of Japanese history, both "*Kojiki*" and "*Nihongi*" mention a gigantic man-eating serpent, with eight heads and eight tails. It is made drunk with vats of saké or rice-beer, one for each head, and when asleep, it is killed by Susano no Mikoto, the brother of Amaterasu, the Sun Goddess. He finds in one of its tails, the wondrous 'Herb-Quelling Sword' which is still preserved as one of the Imperial regalia. This is the first description of an alcoholic beverage, but there are others: sacred saké is served during the reign of the Emperor Suijin, the Empress Jingu wishes long life to the Imperial Prince with saké. The Emperor Ojin receives saké as a tribute from local chieftains. Foreign ambassadors were given sacred saké at the court of Emperor Jomei. But saké, a rice wine as we know it now, was probably made and drunk currently during the reign of the Empress Jito A.D. 687–697. She ascended the throne herself after the death of her husband the Emperor Temmu. She was also the first Japanese sovereign to be cremated in Buddhist ritual.

Saké is the traditional beverage of Japan. Drunk by rich and poor, saké has always been an important factor in the everyday life of the Japanese people, drunk currently among friends or taking an important ritual character at religious ceremonies and festivities. It is made of fermented rice, a single yeast and very pure water, the water being so important that even now trucks are sent to wells and springs known for their purity. Generally saké is put in small individual porcelain bottles (*tokkuri*) and warmed in hot water in a portable copper heater (*shoto*).

Saké cups are usually made of ceramic, lacquer, metal or wood. There is a great variety of recipients for storing and pouring saké: the jars and bottles used (*sakatsubo*) range from the most refined porcelain to rough pottery with the name of the saké shop painted on. Gourds (*hyotan*) left in their natural state were mostly for travelling purposes. There were also elegant cast iron saké kettles, flat in shape with a long, open spout and a lacquered lid, used on formal and festive occasions and for the tea ceremony. Formal cups are very shallow and lacquered red and gold with auspicious symbols or of fine porcelain on a lacquered stand with matching lid. On the rustic side there are the square wooden measures or small bamboo nodes. In the portable lacquer picnic set (*jubako*), the saké bottles are lacquered or made of pewter.

Interesting depictions of saké drinkers in Japanese art are those of the legendary Shojo with long, red hair, shown with a saké jar and bamboo drinking ladle, wearing a saké cup as a hat or sheltering from the rain under a large saké cup. They are also shown dancing round a huge jar or sleeping, head pillowed against the probably empty recipient! As they lived along the seashore, bad fishermen lured these mythical creatures with the irresistible saké, and when they were drunk, captured and killed them to make a beautiful and expensive red dye out of their hair and blood.

In his book T. Kitamura represents a famous Isho *ningyō* (costumed or dressed doll). It is a Noh dancer with the red brocade costume and red wig of the Shojo. The long hair almost touches the ground. The doll was placed at the bedside of children who had smallpox. The spirit causing the disease was afraid of the red coloured hair and clothes and was driven away. The Emperor Kokaku gave this figurine, which is called a Hoso or smallpox doll, to the 25th abbot of Hokyo-ji.*

On a higher level there are the three saké drinkers (*sake-suisan-kyu*). Buddha, Confucius and Lao Tse, happily drinking together from the same jar—and thereby giving an example of peaceful coexistence and showing that the different religions are based on similar principles.

There are yet other motifs linked with saké drinking: the Emperor's three serving men in the Hina Matsuri set show by their expressions the three different effects of over-indulgence: happiness, sadness, and anger; the three ladies-in-waiting (*kanjo*) carry the implements still used at Shinto marriage ceremonies, namely the long-handled gilt saké container (*sashinabe*), the pouring vessel with hinged handle and the presentation tray (*sambo*) with saké cups. Among the miniature furniture there is sometimes included a rectangular, legged tray with a tiered foodbox, a lacquer or pewter saké kettle and three lacquer cups which are still used in Japanese families at New Year for honoured guests.

*Another (contrary) version is that the spirit responsable for smallpox LIKES red-coloured objects, and moves into them, so freeing the sick person from illness.

Okimono / H: 10 cm, W: 9 cm / Ivory, coloured lacquer and lacquer imitating metal / S: Hidemitsu / Makino collection, Tokyo.

The White Horse or Horse of the Gods, an ornament for Boys' Day.

Okimono / H: a. 16 cm, W: 9 cm / Ivory / Late 19th century / Kyoto Gallery, Brussels.

Compact and detailed group representing the Empress Jingu Kogo and her Minister Takenouchi-no-Sukune, holding the infant Emperor Ojin.

Model for okimono / H: 14 cm, W: 6 cm / Wood / S: Mitsunari / Makino collection, Tokyo.

This 'Bijin' or lovely lady is perhaps inspired by woodblock prints, she carries a rigid fan or *uchiwa*. The colours indicate different treatment of surfaces and engraving.

Okimono / H: a. 20 cm, W: a. 7 cm / Ivory / Late 19th century / Kyoto Gallery, Brussels.

Swordsmith and children. The small boy is wearing miniature armour to celebrate Boys' Day.

Monkey Doll/Wood/H: 4cm./S. Masanao.

The *saru ningyō* or monkey doll is defined as a simple rag doll made by young country girls, perhaps inspired by the travelling *sarumawashi* or monkey trainer, with his lively and clever little companion.

The monkey is one of the signs of the oriental Zodiac (a favourable one, the monkey being known for ruse and intelligence), so a refined *netsuke* buyer would prefer the subtle allusion of the doll, to the more common depiction of the real animal. In the medieval period, among the military, there was also a custom of keeping a monkey in the horses' stables, to keep them alert, and possibly, to warn against intruders. This usage could then have led to making monkey dolls for the farms and stables of the countryside, as talismans against evil influences, or as protection for the children who played with them.

Netsuke from the collection of Raymond Bushell (pages 104–106)

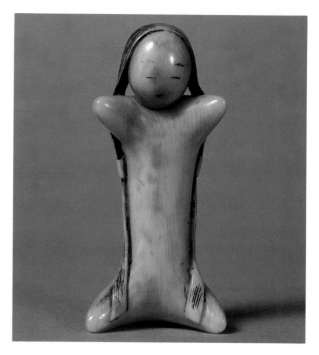

Hoko/Ivory/S. Masanao.

The ancient moon-faced Hoko, made of padded silk, was a protective talisman placed near a newborn child. Illness, possession by evil spirits and future accidents would then be absorbed by the doll.

Tachibina/Carved red lacquer (*tsuishu*)/H: 4.4cm/ Unsigned.

Many layers of red lacquer are applied to a simple wooden base. Each coat must be thoroughly dried and polished, until the required thickness is obtained. The design can then be cut. The original technique of carved lacquer came from China.

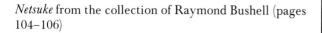

Ichimatsu Doll/Ivory/Cloth arms/Unsigned.

A perfect replica of an unclothed Ichimatsu doll. Head, arms, hands and legs are articulated and the moiré silk joining hands and body is of a type woven during the Edo period.

The expression of this little doll is wistful, and it is evident that a master's hand has conveyed its message.

Nara Doll/Kasuga dragon god/Painted cypress wood/H: 5.9cm/S. Morikawa Toen.

This *netsuke* was made by the greatest carver of Nara *ningyō*, Morikawa Toen (1820–1894), who brought the art of the Nara doll to its highest peak. He has combined technique (*ittōbori*) and colouring, more as a sculptor and painter, than as a dollmaker. No other artist has ever captured the real spirit of the Noh theatre so completely as Morikawa Toen in his colourful and bewitching miniature personages.

After The Bath/Colours on *gofun*/Unsigned.

This miniature girl-child is an unusual *netsuke* indeed. It is undoubtedly inspired by the white-skinned and big-headed Gosho dolls, covered with polished *gofun*. It is a humorous interpretation, for by all rules, the Gosho doll should be a small boy.

Dairibina/Body, gold lacquer/Face/Ivory/Unsigned.

This small seated Emperor, a figure of the Hina Matsuri set, could have been executed by an *inro* maker, as part of a gold lacquered set, combining *netsuke*, *ojime*, and *inro*, decorated with related motifs. In this figurine more importance has been given to the lacquering than to the carving, which speaks for the above theory.

Uji Tea Picker / Coloured teawood / Unsigned.

A tea picker doll, carved in typical *ittōbori* or one-knife technique.

It is more refined than the usual examples. The thickness of the layers of colour, the soft, dark hues, have made the contours more rounded, more smooth and supple, and the years of use have imparted a beautiful patina and an indefinable glow.

Uji Tea Picker / Coloured pottery (earthenware) / Brand of Otowa, a kiln used by Kyoto potters. / S. Ken (KEN'YA).

This pottery *netsuke* simulates the wooden Uji *ningyō*. The copying of other materials was a favourite (if difficult) trick of *netsuke* and lacquer artists, and served as proof of mastery and virtuosity in their art. It is part of Japanese refinement to make a costly material look like a simple one, thus, ivory can be made to imitate wood or deerhorn.

Imari / H:6 cm, DM: 15 cm / Porcelain / 18th century / Private collection.

Wide, shallow bowl decorated with overglaze enamels in red, gold and green and a delicate underglaze blue and white pattern on footring and inside. Three fan-shaped reserves show Tachibina dolls among coloured maple leaves, symbolizing spring and autumn.

'Fallen Tachibina—as far from spring as autumn leaves'

Imari / H: 24 cm, W: 12 cm / Porcelain / 17th century / Kyoto Gallery, Brussels.

Figure of a nobleman wearing a formal robe (*kami-shimo*) decorated in overglaze enamels with orange and gold prunus flowers, green and black bamboo leaves, and pale, mauve clouds. Hair and belt are black. On the shoulders of his *kami-shimo*, the *mon* or heraldic device of his family is visible.

Hirado / Cups: H: 6 cm, DM: 4 cm / H: 3.5 cm, DM: 5.5 cm / Bottle: H: 14 cm, W: 6 cm / Porcelain, *some-tsuke*: blue on white underglaze / Cups: Hirado Gasho (a Living Cultural Asset) / Private collection.

The two saké cups are decorated with a design of *karako* (Chinese children) The saké bottle is in the form of a Kokeshi doll, the top of the head serves as a saké cup.

Mashiko / H: 11cm, W: 13 cm / Earthenware with touches of grey and black glazing / INSCR: Mashiko / Private collection.

Lidded pot representing the head of a Kokeshi doll.

Wood-block print / H: 12 cm, W: 17 cm / Private collection.

Double wood-block print by Kunisada, also known as Toyokuni III (1786–1864) representing a handsome man showing a Tachibina to a richly dressed young lady. It is a parody of *'The Tale of Genji'*. The background is embossed. It is possible that the print was meant to be cut in half, and was part of a game (like the shell game) consisting of pairs which went together, or a book cover.

Wood-block print / Unsigned / Private collecion.

Gosho doll-children playing with hobby horses (*haru koma*). The ox-cart and wisteria flowers are emblems of nobility and spring. The print illustrates the story of Yoritomo's two famous horses, one white and one black. Yoritomo gave the black horse to Kajiwara Kagesue and the white horse to Sasaki Takatsune, his generals. When the army came to the Uji river, Kajiwara galloped away to meet the foe, but Sasaki called out: 'Take care, your girth is loose!' So he was the first to meet the enemy, and the white horse won the race.

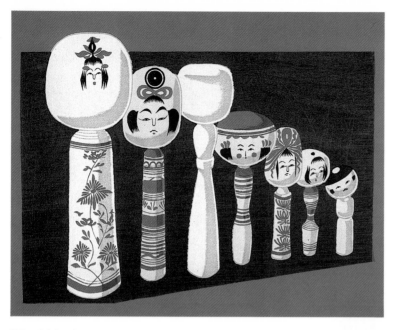

Wood-block print / H: 32 cm, W: 23 cm / Unsigned / Gift of Magatani Antiques, Tokyo.

This amusing print shows a fanciful and surrealistic Kokeshi doll. It is of a non-existant species, a delightful mixture of unknown origin. A male Kokeshi, some parts carved in *ittōbori* manner as in Nara dolls, the limbs attached with textile joints like the Ichimatsu, a forehead pattern sometimes found on Gosho dolls, a plum and a cherry flower decoration, reminiscent of Hina dolls! Is this rare specimen a doll collector's dream—or nightmare?

It is certainly the anti-kokeshi—it is everything a true Kokeshi doll should NOT be!

Wood-block print / H: 23 cm, W: 32 cm / Unsigned / Gift of Magatani Antiques, Tokyo.

A row of seven Kokeshi dolls, which can be identified by their characteristic shapes and patterns. From left to right:

1. Narugo—a sturdy doll with a large head, which squeaks when turned; squared shoulders and a chrysanthemum pattern on the body.
2. Tsuchiyu—a slim body with circular lines and a head decorated with concentric black circles and a red bow.
3. Nambu or Hanamaki—a colourless wooden doll called *kinakina*.
4. Yajiro—a cap-like head pattern, circular lines on a waisted body and single-lid eyes.
5. Togatta—a red radial design on the head and layered chrysanthemums on the body.
6. Yamagata—Sakunami (?)—dominant colours red and green and a tuft of black hair on the head.
7. Nambu or Hanamaki—a mobile head.

Kabuki dancer / H: 24 cm, W: 15 cm / Collection J. Steylaerts, Belgium.

Ishobina or costume doll representing a Kabuki dancer (*kagamijishi*). The face has delicately painted and modelled features and inlaid glass eyes. The costume is made of three kinds of richly and differently patterned gold brocade, lined with beige silk. The long white wig is made of animal hair.

Wood-block print / H: 35 cm, W: 24 cm / S: Kuni-chika / Collection P. de Klark, Belgium.

The Kabuki actor Kawarazaki in the role of Musashi-bo-Benkei in 'Kanjincho' (The Subscription List).

Kabuki actor / enlargement of the head / Kyoto Gallery, Brussels.

An Ishobina or costume doll figure of a Kabuki actor playing the role of Benkei in 'The Subscription List'. He is wearing the costume of a travelling monk or *yamabushi*.

Scene of Kanjincho / Two standing actors: H: a. 20 cm / Sitting actor: H: a. 15 cm / Kyoto Gallery, Brussels.

Katagami / Stencil for resist dyeing / Maker: Hajime Kobayashi / Private collection.

Four small boys in the form of Gosho dolls, playing with a kite or *tako*. Flying kites is a typical New Year's pastime for boys. The kite carries auspicious characters *Ryu*, *tatsu* (dragon). A stencil of this kind would be used for decoration of a child's festival *kimono*.

Silk fabric / H: 30 cm, W: 28 cm / Private collection.

Such textiles were used to make children's *kimono* for special occasions, such as Girls' Day and shrine visits. Gosho doll-children are playing games, upper right with an *ito-mari* or thread ball, lower right with a *hagoita* or battledore.

Silk fabric / H: 23 cm, W: 28 cm / Private collection.

Detail of the lining of a *haori* or short silk jacket worn over a *kimono*. A boy Gosho doll is pulling a wheeled treasure ship (*takarabune*) filled with precious things — coral, pearls, the hat of invisibility, cloisonné. His bolero is decorated with auspicious symbols and he is surrounded by other toys. Note the Nara dolls representing Jo and Uba, the happy old couple of Takasago (middle, under).

Kanagu / H: 2 cm, W: 4 cm / S: Isho / Private collection.

A tobacco pouch clasp, showing Tachibina, clam shells and cherry blossom. *Shakudo*, gold and silver have been harmoniously combined.

Kanagu / H: 2.5 cm, W: 4.5 cm / S: Taminori / Private collection.

This clasp is of most refined execution, it shows a puppeteer manipulating a stick puppet on a stand. *Shakudo*, *shibuichi*, gold, silver and copper create depth and colour.

Girls' Day doll / H: 15 cm, W: 18 cm / Collection Luc and Jessie Sanders, Belgium.

Lady-in-waiting (*kanjo*)

Saké set and tiered food-box on tray / Miniature doll's furniture / Tray: H: 3 cm, W: 8 cm, L: 16 cm / Red, black and gold lacquer on wooden base.   Pewter saké kettle. / Late 19th century / White Art Centre, Ghent, Belgium.

These utensils were kept for happy occasions and show auspicious symbols such as the crane and pine, emblems of longevity.   The smallest saké cup has a diameter of 2 cm.   Some old *hina* sets have dozens of tiny accessories.

Saké cup / H: 1.5 cm, W: 6 cm / Wooden base, red and gold lacquer / Private collection.

Decorated with the Tachibina pair, a willow branch and camellias. The weeping willow is the emblem of feminine grace, gentleness and spring. The subject is an allusion to an old and well-known folk-song that begins:

Ah, the jewel-like camellia
And the jewel-like willow
That grow in Takasago
Upon Saisago Hill..........

Tanzaku (poem card) / H: 36 cm, W: 6 cm / Signed and seal / Private collection.

Painted on silk stiffened with cardboard, the *tanzaku* is a modest version of a hanging scroll. A specific wooden holder was used for hanging seasonal pictures and poems on the wall or in the *tokonoma*. This one was obviously used in spring and the third month. *Tanzaku* also had a special storage box, long and narrow, made of wood, silk covered or embellished with lacquer.

Daruma / Okimono / H: 15 cm, W: 8 cm / Keyaki root-wood / Private collection.

Head and shoulders are carved in the *ittōbori* technique (one-knife carving). The robe is suggested by the natural curve of the rough wood.

Daruma / H: 6 cm, W: 7 cm / Ash-tray, rosewood, ivory teeth and tortoiseshell eyes / Private collection.

Daruma / H: 4 cm, W: 4.5 cm / *Netsuke*, lacquered wood, ivory and coral inlay / S: 'Hideyuki' in gold seal / Private collection.

Imari / H: 4.5 cm, DM: 4 cm / Porcelain / *Onna* Daruma / H: 7 cm, W: 5 cm / Matsuyama / Both private collection.

Saké cup decorated with three *Onna* or Women Daruma, respectively in orange, gold and orange (overglaze), grey and black (underglaze) and various other toys. The souvenir doll with silk hair and painted features, is wrapped in red and white crêpe and beige and gold brocade.

PART III
MISCELLANEA

PUPPETS

Puppets, articulated and movable dolls, were introduced to Japan from Korea, China, and other Asian countries in the course of the 9th century. Rudimentary puppets or *kugutsu* (the earliest word for puppet) existed prior to this date, used for the amusement of children. The first travelling puppeteers (*kugutsumawashi*) were probably Korean immigrants judging by the costumes represented on old documents, and their puppets quite small for convenient transportation.

Beggars and peddlers crossed the countryside, visiting villages and farms, putting on shows to attract sales or alms. Dolls, prints, and other objects exist showing the puppeteer with his puppets or the monkey trainer (*sarumawashi*) with his monkey. This raises an interesting point: a rag doll in the simplified shape of a monkey, was formerly made in certain regions of Japan. The monkey, an unusual and intriguing animal could well have been the model for the *saru ningyō* or monkey doll.

The amusing little plays formed a rare and welcome attraction in the everyday life of the inhabitants of distant and lonely settlements. As the itinerant show was usually a one-man business, the puppets were small and actioned by the inserted hands and fingers (*yubi* and *tezuma ningyō*) or with sticks. The stage was a portable oblong box carried round the neck with a broad band reaching to the waist, leaving the hands free. The dolls could also be packed in this box. Various other forms of puppetry were practised by travelling puppeteers (marionettes or string puppets and rod puppets).

In the early Momoyama period (1568–1603) performances were given in the precincts of temples and shrines, they were often religious or moralizing in content. At that time, accompanied by music and song, the larger dolls were manipulated above a horizontal screen, behind which the manipulators were hidden from the viewers. From religious and moral lessons for illiterate people emerged the Joruri (later named Bunraku) puppet theatre, a popular divertissement for the townspeople.

The three most important components of Joruri are the puppets and the mastery with which they are manipulated, the virtuosity of recital of a highly stylized text (the actual Joruri) and the enhancing effect of the *samisen* music which accompanies the acts. Joruri drama gained enormously in popularity when the music of the *samisen* (a three-stringed instrument from the Ryukyu Islands (Okinawa)), was used to underline the action. In its definite form Joruri knew its hour of glory due to the efforts of three men: the brilliant and talented playwright Chikamatsu Monzaemon (1653–1725) who wrote 120 plays for the puppet theatre, and the reciter Takemoto Gidayu (1651–1714) whose style and voice were so distinctive, that a dramatic form of narration was named after him; Tachimatsu Hachirobei elaborated a new method of manipulation in full view of the audience.

By 1727 the puppets made on the Island of Awaji, in the Inland Sea, had reached a high degree of perfection. They were now equipped with a sophisticated system of sticks, strings and springs, actioning mobile eyes, eyebrows and mouths which permitted more expressive acting, they also had articulated hands and fingers for gesturing and holding accessories. They even had interchangeable heads for a rapid change of expression or personality.

These puppets were manipulated by three operators, a master dressed in formal costume who worked the head and right arm, retaining a face devoid of all expression throughout the performance; two assistants, hooded and totally dressed in black (colour of invisibility) one working the left arm, the other the feet. An interesting feature of these puppets is that the left arm is longer than the right because the operator of the left arm must stand farther away from the puppet, to leave more room for the head operator. These are the refined versions of more rustic Awaji puppets, which were first used to tour the country by hawkers, amateurs and propagators of Jodo Buddhism, and in their final perfected form became the Bunraku puppets with their own fixed theatres, plays and enthusiasts in the great towns of Kyoto, Osaka and Edo. Among these the Bunraku-za of Osaka was the most famous.

For some time, *ningyō-shibai* or doll theatres rivalled with and even outclassed Kabuki. They lost much of their popularity when their plays and acting conventions were taken over by the Kabuki theatre. Most Kabuki plays were originally written for the small actors with wooden heads and a life conferred on them by human virtuosity. Other particular forms of puppet expression existed, practised from time to time but not possessing permanent theatres or great popularity, such as *noroma ningyō* or comic puppets (conceived by Noromatsu Kambei) and *kuruma ningyō*—the operator propelling himself about the stage seated in a wheeled box.

KOBE NINGYŌ

From a relatively cheap souvenir (an ordinary sailor could buy one along the docks), to an exceedingly rare collector's item, lies but a time-span of a hundred years! Kobe mechanical dolls take their name from the Port of Kobe, where they were made from 1870 to 1920. Quaint little keepsakes, amusing toys, but never highly regarded during the short period of their manufacture, they are now sold for unbelievable prices which would have astounded their former creators and made

them extremely rich and happy! Not many original specimens are to be found anywhere in the world today, except in museums and private collections.

The small wooden figures are simply hand-carved and the colours subdued—natural wood, blackened, or small pieces of ebony, inlaid bone or ivory eyes, and a very wide, red mouth (when open). Most parts are mobile, and heads, arms and mouths are actioned by an intricate and ingenious system of wheels, pulleys, and strings when a knob is manually turned. The co-ordination of all the movements is perfect, and one can only marvel at the hours of patient labour which must have been necessary for the production of just one figure.

There is no attempt at aesthetic effect—movement is the primary purpose—and usually the toy simply consists of one or more torsos on top of a small box in which the mechanism is concealed. The makers represented a Negroid type of head (black, round, white eyes, broad nose) as they probably did not want to portray their own countrymen, nor the foreigners for whom the souvenirs were intended.*

The survivors of the hazards of travel, destructive children, uncaring adults, and general catastrophes, have a perfect right to pride of place in the discerning doll collector's 'imaginary museum'.

* Possibly inspired by Negro sailors, who disembarked in Kobe, when the port was re-opened in 1868.

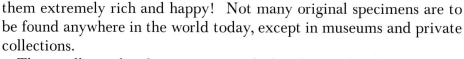

KARAKURI

The first mention of a moving figure is found in the 'Nihongi', for the year A.D. 658, when the Buddhist priest Chiyū made a 'Shinan-sha' or south-pointing chariot. It was a miniature device consisting of a pointing figure on a small horse-drawn cart. The outstretched arm of the mobile passenger unfailingly indicated the south. As the Chinese Emperor had always to face south, even while travelling, it is certain that the invention was due to Chinese immigrants, this chariot having been known in China from the fifth century BC. The above-mentioned priest Chiyū, presented a 'Shinan-sha' to the Japanese Emperor, Tenchi, in 666. It has been erroneously called a compass, however, the driving force was NOT magnetism, but an ingenious mechanism. The 'Konjaku Monogatari' also records a mechanical construction to water fields, in the shape of a human being, (mizugoi ningyō), ordered by Prince Kōjōin in 850.

The dolls which are at present termed Karakuri ningyō or trick dolls (from the verb karakuru=to trick), are usually automated manually or by a wind system, and in the broad sense of the word include the Kobe *ningyō*, single dolls with built-in moving power, single dolls and groups on stands hiding the mechanism, and also the festival puppets or '*dashi karakuri*', large articulated puppets used on '*dashi*', the ceremonial floats or chariots, drawn through the streets on the occasion of annual religious festivals of Shinto origin. The operators are hidden inside the vehicles and the movements of the dolls ingeniously coordinated by means of metal and wooden bars, wheels, and strong silk cables. Most *dashi ningyō* have the features and clothes of *karako* or Chinese children, an indication that the first jugglers and acrobats were Chinese. (See Takeda.)

The small *karakuri* dolls on stands, in which the wind mechanism was hidden, were generally made for the privileged class; these automats are named '*zashiki karakuri*', the imported European clocks (1550) and their intricate design furnishing a further source of inspiration to improve later development and performance. When exactly *zashiki karakuri* dolls originated in the Tokugawa period (1615–1868) is not certain, but there is a dated example (1713) of a cherry blossom viewing dance with different costume dolls performing on a stand. A perfected and most sophisticated system of springs, wheels, balanced weights (even sand and water), force of gravity and mercury pressure, make these articulated dolls into somersaulting acrobats, energetic dancers and musicians, or tea servers (*chahakobi*), who walk the length of a table to bring a cup of tea, stop when the cup is lifted, turn and return to their sender when the cup is replaced. At present, dollmakers can reconstruct the tea-serving doll, using eighteenth century technical documents to guide them.

As the first Japanese clocks were made in Nagoya, it is not surprising that this town was also the centre of Zashiki and Dashi *karakuri* production, and that most 'Dashi festivals' are in the Nagoya area. There are today, a hundred and eighty-one chariots and approximately 398 Dashi *karakuri ningyō* in existence. The *ningyō* of the Zashiki type are extremely rare, especially in working order, and can only be found in museums and private collections.

The first English language catalogue describing *dashi karakuri* puppets was recently published by the Japan Foundation and Barbican Art Gallery, on the occasion of an exceptional exhibition at the Barbican Centre, London. This was the first time *dashi karakuri ningyō* had been shown outside Japan.

TERU-TERU BŌZU—
It never rains—it pours!

A magic doll, a folk doll—if you have planned a picnic, an outing or any other activity that requires a clear and sunny day and it has been raining so long that you are thinking, like Noah, of building your private ark, take heart and make *teru-teru bōzu* instead. A square piece of white cotton or paper, stuffing for a round head, a piece of string tied under the chin, a smiling face drawn on—and behold—we have worked magic! We have made a doll that will stop the rain and make the sun come out to smile back at our naive little ghost. For best results, it should be hung under the eaves or on a branch, with a pure heart and a rock-fast faith! *Teru-teru bōzu* means 'shine, shine, shaven head' and refers to the shaven heads of Buddhist monks. It comes to mind, that as Jizo is invoked to bring rain by immersing his statue in the river or rubbing mud on his face, it is quite possible that he can also stop the rain, especially if the children he loves so much, ask him this favour! Could it be that this simple rag or paper doll is an old country version of the friendly Buddhist bonze?

IZUMEKO

The people of the northern prefectures of Honshu, especially the farming families working in fields and woods, took along their babies, and to keep them out of harm, wrapped them up snugly in a coverlet or old *futon* and put them in a large basket, in an upright position. The mothers, busy at home, did the same and tied small toys to the edge of the basket, for the children to play with. In Narugo and Tsuruoka, dolls representative of this custom are still being made. They range from Emperor and Empress pairs, wrapped in brocade, to miniatures sitting in chestnut husks and acorn cups.

HAGOITA

As the flying of kites is a typical New Year's pastime for boys, so the playing of *hanetsuki* is the game for girls. The result for the loser is a black spot on the face! It is the Japanese version of battledore (*hagoita*) and shuttlecock (*hane*). The *hane* is a berry or little ball with implanted feathers. The game is a Chinese legacy, dating from the 14th century. The aristocracy played this genteel game, when they were presented with artistically lacquered and painted examples by their carpenters, as New Year gifts. Later, simplified versions were sold at shrines, as talismanic protection against fire, a much feared catastrophy in Japanese towns and villages. (carpenter=wood=fire).

Even earlier, the *hagoita* had antecedents in the Heian period, when it was used for exorcism and warding off evil generally. At the Sagichō ceremony, held in the grounds of the Imperial palace, on the fifteenth day of the first lunar month, old documents, letters, fans, New Year decorations and *hagoita* were burnt on a fire of new bamboo. This ritual was meant to destroy the bad influences of the past year and bring prosperity for the coming year, and to prevent bad luck, such as fires, earthquakes and illness. This usage also explains the fact that few authentic old *hagoita* have survived. The custom has been kept to this day, and many temples throughout Japan burn old toys and dolls.

Hagoita became most popular when makers with commercial flair began decorating them with wood-block print models of beautiful women (*bijin*) and Kabuki actors. The employed technique is called *oshi-e;* it was also used for making various personages on sticks (*oshiebina*), for play or decoration. On elaborate *hagoita*, up to 50 pieces are cut out, padded, glued, and covered with a dazzling variety of textiles; colourful silks and gold brocades combined, create the lavish and rich effects of the Kabuki costumes in all their splendour. The faces and hands are painted on silk, and loose elements such as fans, flowers, swords and pieces of armour, add to the relief of the piece.

These *hagoita* are too ornate and too heavy to play with and mostly bought as presents for new-born girls or as New Year decoration for the *tokonoma*. Shopkeepers like to show them in their windows during the festive season, and vie with each other for the biggest and most expensive ones, as the size is believed to be in direct proportion to the prosperity of the shop. While some shrines still sell the simply painted old types (Kagoshima, Fukushima, Hiroshima), as souvenirs and lucky charms, the most famous *hagoita* fair or *hagoita-ichi* is held on December 17th, 18th and 19th at Asakusa Kannon Temple in Tokyo. Stalls showing sizes ranging from miniatures to giants of more than one meter high, make a memorable and rainbow-hued panorama, in the grounds of the temple at twilight, and draw huge crowds. The sale of a particularly large and expensive *hagoita* is applauded enthusiastically by the delighted spectators.

WARA NINGYŌ

The interesting double wood-block print by Toyokuni III (1786–1864), consists of the front and back cover pages of a story book ('*Shiranui*'). Melodramatic tales of love, murder, revenge and sorcery, were popular in the Edo period. By showing a critical moment of the action, the cover was meant to excite the curiosity of the buyer. The woman is holding a Wara *ningyō* or straw doll. Here it is obviously a fetish, being used to cause pain and death. Death will follow, when the fourth nail is plunged into the straw figure. The words four and death (*shi*) are phonetically the same, and are as superstitiously regarded in Japan, as thirteen in the West. The woman is clenching with her teeth, the wooden hammer with which the man could strike the Buddhist bell placed on her *obi* and possibly break the evil spell. She is probably a seductive lady, as an untied *obi* and a red underrobe are unmistakable erotic symbols. Revenge for a murdered father, brother, or lover—jealousy because the man has left her for another love, are usually the themes of such stories.

There formerly existed a strange custom concerning Wara *ningyō*. When two people of the same family died within the same year it was believed that a third would inevitably die, if a Wara doll was not put in a miniature coffin and buried under a small tombstone (*ningyō-no-haka*) bearing a *kaimyo* or posthumous Buddhist name. Niigata Prefecture still produces decorative straw animals, and perhaps even the Japanese have forgotten their primary purpose. They were intended as presents for the dead at the time of O-Bon, the Festival of the Dead: Wara *uma*—straw horses for the dead to ride, and Wara *ushi*—oxen to work for them in the Valley of the Shadow of Death. They could also be a naive derivation and adaptation of Haniwa figures.

Etching / H: 17.5 cm, W: 12.5 cm / Private collection.

Bunraku puppet by the famous contemporary artist Nishisawa Shizuo, born 1912. This artist is obsessed by the Bunraku theatre and the majority of his prints feature puppets in their own silent and mysterious world of rich colours.

Stick puppet / H: 40 cm, W: 20 cm / Collection Luc and Jessie Sanders, Belgium.

This puppet is a reduction of the one-third life-size real Bunraku puppet. The head and arms are attached to sticks and the hand can be inserted inside the body.   He is evidently an important personage, dressed in formal court dress (*kami-shimo*) of brilliant gold brocade — the underrobe of painted silk.

Wood-block print / H: 18 cm, W: 12 cm / Private collection.

The picture, by Toyokuni III, shows a travelling woman puppeteer, manipulating two *karako* or Chinese children, playing the cymbals. They are Tezuma *ningyō* or hand puppets. She is wearing a *kimono*, unusually decorated with folded paper (*origami*) boats. At New Year, she was often accompanied by a male partner, hidden under a long robe, who worked a lion mask with mobile jaws, while executing the dance of the lion or *shi-shi mai*. The background is patterned with ox-cart wheels in water, a decorative motif dating from the Heian period. The wheels were soaked to keep them from drying, cracking or warping. Here they could be a subtle allusion to the Year of the Ox.

Wood-block print / H: 24 cm, W: 18 cm / By Kunichika / Printed in 1866 / Private collection.

Puppeteer with a warrior puppet (a string and rod mechanism is visible behind the feet and legs). The title reads *Chushingura* (The 47 Ronin) while the puppet shown is Benkei with his seven weapons.

Kobe ningyō / H: 9 cm, W: 7 cm / Late 19th century / Ebony, various woods, inlaid bone eyes / Private collection.

Three photographs showing different phases of movement: the happy tippler is: 1) pouring saké, 2) lifting the flask or *tokkuri* and opening his mouth, 3) dropping the flask, bending his head, lifting the cup, and drinking.

Karakuri (automat) / H: 23 cm, W: 19 cm / Early 18th century / Costume doll on stand containing the mechanism / Oyama collection, Tokyo.

This happy juggler is now resting, but when he was young, while turning round and round, he threw the ball from fan to hat for the amusement of young and old. The large painted base with the traditional painted reserve (*kozama*), hides the wind mechanism.

Ningyo—Mermaid / H: 6 cm, W: 4 cm / Netsuke, ivory, colours and tortoiseshell inlay / S: Koraku / Private collection.

Anesama / H: 25 cm, W: 9 cm / Private collection.

Paper doll (literally: elder sister) made in all parts of Japan, making clever use of patterned (*chiyogami*) and plain (*irogami*) paper. A creative pastime for many ladies, showing fashions and hairstyles of all periods of Japanese history. Characteristically, this doll has no features.

Teru Teru Bozu / H: 25 cm, W: 15 cm.

Paper or rag doll hung outside to stop the rain (Folk custom)

Izumeko / H: 12 cm, W: 9 cm / Kimekomi / Private collection.

The dolls illustrate an old custom of wrapping up babies and putting them in baskets while the parents were working. This elaborate pair can be used as Emperor and Empress dolls for Girls' Day. The heads are *gofun* covered and the hair is made of silk.

Hagoita / H: 120 cm, W: 50 cm / Private collection.

A giant *hagoita*, showing a battle scene. It is a complicated and baroque piece, filled with as much movement and rich colours as a Kabuki play. From the size it can be deducted that it was bought for a very prosperous shop indeed!

Structure of costume doll / H: 35 cm, W: 13 cm / Wood, *gofun*, silk hair and rush body. Contemporary/ Private collection.

The head of old dolls was inserted in the body with a wooden peg, or head and peg were of one piece. Sometimes a metal pin was used. The hair is made of silk, the glass eyes are incrusted. The head carries a small illegible stamp of the maker.

Wood-block print / H: 17 cm, W: 23 cm / Private collection.

The front and back cover pages of a book. The print is by Toyokuni III (1786–1864). The woman is depicted holding a *wara ningyō* or straw doll, here used as a fetish for casting an evil spell. A dramatic moment is shown to excite the curiosity of the reader.

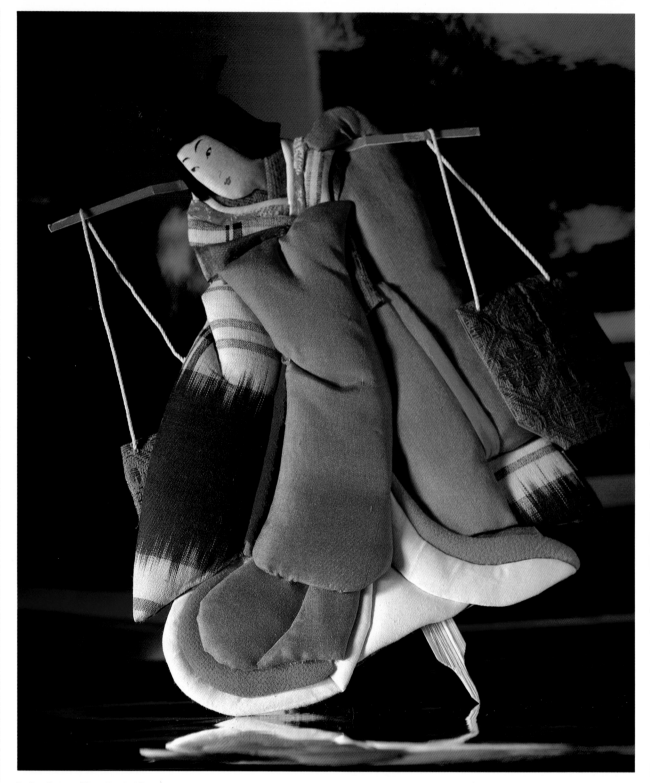

Oshiebina (Stick doll) / H: 30 cm, W: 21 cm / Private collection.

Padded silk of many hues forms the clothes, the features are delicately painted. The doll can be pegged into a thickly woven *tatami* mat, a wooden stand or the ground, with the pointed bamboo stick. Matsumoto was the chief production centre of these dolls during the first quarter of the nineteenth century, counting hundreds of different personages. The figure represents a *shiokumi-onna* or woman salt-carrier. She transports buckets of brine for the extraction of salt. A story tells of young Lord Yukihira, who saw two such beautiful young sisters working by the seashore. He fell in love with both, and loved them equally.

148

Index

★Bold numbers refer to colour plates.